CONTENTS

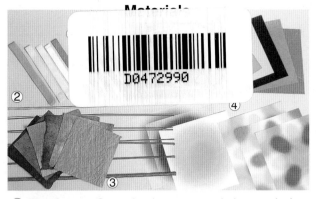

Materials

① **Floral tape:** Several colors are needed not only for making stems but also small centers of flowers.

② **Wrapped floral wire:** #14, #18, #20, #24 (The larger the number, the thinner the wire) are used in this book, as well as thick ¼ " and ⅛ "(diameter) types, wrapped with thicker layers of greenish paper.

③ ***Washi* paper:** All leaves and some flowers in this book are made of this fibrous Japanese paper, for more delicate expressions in color and shape. To use this paper as origami paper, cut precisely into desired squares.

④ **Origami paper:** 6 " square sheets of origami paper in assorted colors are most common, although other types are used in this book, such as shaded-colored and double-sided paper. When materials call for alcohol-based marker, it is recommended that you color a part or both sides of white paper for more effect.

Tools

① **Rulers:** Straight and triangle.

② **Paper glue:** Any type of paper glue is suitable for pasting origami paper.

③ **Wood glue:** This book uses wood glue, which turns clear when dried.

④ **Metal snips:** A pair of cutting pliers can also do the job.

⑤ **Paper clips:** These clips are convenient to secure parts to be attached.

⑥ **Alcohol-based markers:** Sold under the names of Maxon or Copic, these felt-tip pens are handy because the ink penetrates through the paper, coloring both sides simultaneously. Also, colors do not darken, even when applied in layers. If unavailable, use permanent markers.

⑦ **Scissors:** We recommend that you use two pairs, one for cutting paper, and the other for floral tape, since the tape may leave the blades sticky.

ROSE

Backside view of the blossom
(The same calyx/cup is used
for all types of roses.)

#1 The inner and outer folds create the rose
petals' light and shaded regions.
See page 39 for instructions.

#2 These flamboyant blossoms are constructed with four
layers of folded squares. See page 42 for instructions.

Smaller blossoms using two layers

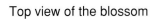

#3 *Washi* paper adds a delicate shading and texture to rose, the queen of flowers. See page 40 for instructions.

HYACINTH

Star-like, crumpled florets are made of origami paper precut into hexagons.
See page 44 for instructions.

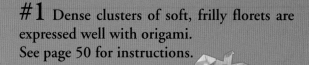
#1 Dense clusters of soft, frilly florets are expressed well with origami.
See page 50 for instructions.

#2 A branched and delicate-looking version made of the same florets as in #1.
See page 50 for instructions.

Close-up of the florets

5

TULIP

All blossoms are made of white paper which has been colored with color-penetrating markers. See page 53 for instructions.

Top view of the blossom

Backside view of the blossom

Close-up of the buds and blossom

CARNATION

The delicate, frilly petals of the carnation are created with neatly folded tissue paper.
See page 46 for instructions.

VIOLET

The violet blossom is attached at an angle to the calyx(cup).

Each petal has its own shape in this fragile spring flower.
See page 48 for instructions.

PANSY

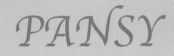

Backside view of the blossom

Each of these expressive pansy blossoms is made out of a single sheet of origami. Notice two different petal shapes.

See page 36 for instructions.

PANSY

NARCISSUS

#1 Simple yet artistic, both the yellow and white blossoms are made of the same yellow origami. See page 54 for instructions.

#2 Some additional folds to the petals create a sence of depth in this version. See page 56 for instructions.

Backside view of the blossom #1

DOKUDAMI

This 3D blossom may require a little technique, but it is worth the effort. See page 58 for instructions.

Side view of the blossom

Backside view of the blossom

CINERARIA

Close-up of the blossom

The centers and tips of the petals are colored to create a realistic effect. One blossom needs only one sheet of paper. See page 60 for instructions.

Close-up of the blossom

POLYANTHUS PRIMROSE

These bright and cheery blossoms are enhanced with yellow centers, which are glued on before folding. See page 62 for instructions.

#2 Only one sheet of origami is used to create each flower head. You can mix and match the colors of centers and petals. See page 66 for instructions.

Backside view of the calyx(cup)

GERBERA

Close-up of the double-flowering blossom

#1 Narrow-petal garberas using single or double layers of origami. See page 64 for instructions.

ZINNIA

Close-up of the blossom

The hemispheric flower head, closely packed with pointed petals, can be a lovely decoration for a gift box. See page 70 for instructions.

Elegant irises in a purplish blend are distinguished further by a fold - and-curve technique. See page 78 for instructions.

Side view of the blossom, showing how the calyx(cup) is attached

HOLLYHOCK

For best results, crease the pleats sharply. See page 80 for instructions.

Side view of the blossom showing how the calyx(cup) is attached

HYDRANGEA

Florets of various sizes are assembled to create a natural look. See page 82 for instructions.

The "fertile blossoms" in the center are embellished effectively. See page 83 for instructions.

Showing how to assemble the florets

LACE CAP HYDRANGEA

BLUE STAR

The cute, star-shaped florets are made out of small origami that are precut into pentagons. See page 84 for instructions.

Close-up of the buds, calyxes and blossoms

White sheets of paper are partially colored to express the refreshing tones of morning glory.
See page 74 for instructions.

Side view of the blossoms and bud, showing how the calyxes are attached

MORNING GLORY

BEGONIA

The yellow centers can be made by either attaching a small piece of paper, or simply using color-gradated origami. See page 86 for instructions.

Assembly of the florets

SUNFLOWER

A large sheet of *washi* paper is used to reallistically recreate the size of the sunflower. See page 71 for instructions.

Close-up of the bud

Side view of the blossom

DAHLIA

The tubular petals of the dahlia are made in an expressive way by using gradated origami. See page 76 for instructions.

Close-up of the opening blossom

#1 Six-petal clematis using crimson colored origami. The stamens are made of smaller sheet glued to the center. See page 98 for instructions.

Close-up of the clematis #2

#2 A rounded petal version of #1. The center is colored with a color marker. See page 99 for instructions.

CLEMATIS

#4 A broader petal version of #3.
Colored and shaded origami gives an
elegant expression.
See page 97 for instructions.

#3 An eight-petal version of clematis
blossom, shaded with color markers.
See page 96 for instructions.

LILY

The trumpet figure of a lily is created with only one sheet of paper. Set the blossoms as if they are bowing to in all directions. See page 102 for instructions.

Close-up of the bud

Side view of the blossom

#1 The unique structure of the "lip petal" is well expressed with a small sheet of origami added. See page 88 for instructions.

Close-up of the blossom #2

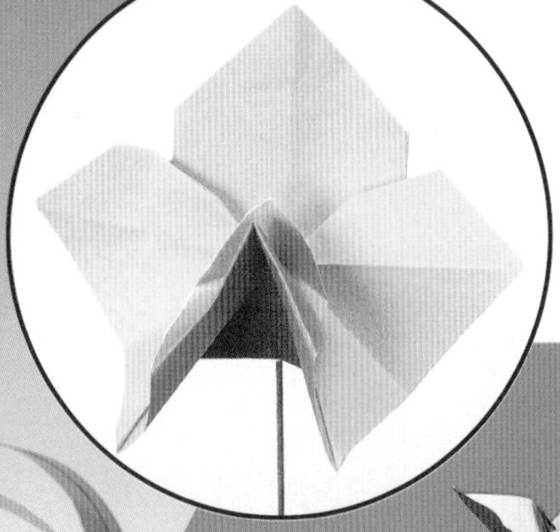

#2 A fuller impression is achieved by adding another fold to each of the #1 florets. See page 90 for instructions

Close-up of the blossom #3

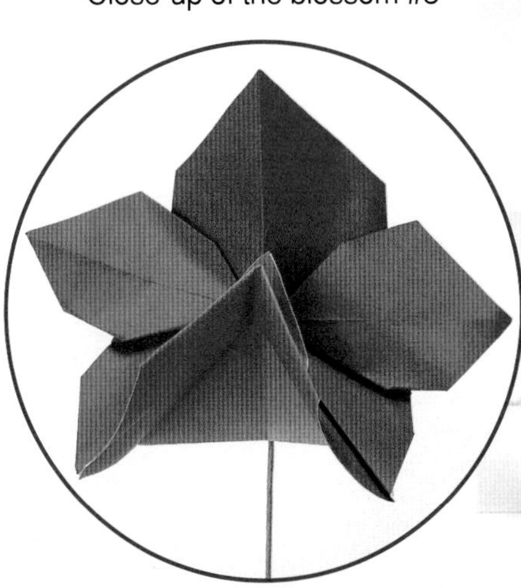

#3 Each of the little petals are rounded by folding the corners under. See page 91 for instructions.

Close-up of each
stage of the flower

Side view of
the blossom

SPRAY MUM

Octagonally cut origami in striking color
creates a vivid look of the mum. See page
93 for instructions.

CHRYSANTHEMUM

Backside view of the blossom

CORNFLOWER

Close folding of origami defines the
tubular petals of chrysanthemums.
See page 105 for instructions.

Side view of the blossom

Attach thin stems to focus on the lightness of fine
petals of the cornflowers. See page 104 for instructions.

Backside view of the blossom, showing how the calyx is attached

COSMOS

A single sheet of paper makes the petals and the center at the same time. See page 68 for instructions.

#1 Two sheets of origami are glued together for a color effect. See page 106 for instructions.

BALLOON FLOWER

Side view of the blossom
#1 and #2

Close-up of the blossom #2

#2 The white and blue blossoms have less pointed petals than those of the pink ones. Use either a single sheet or double layers. See page 107 for instructions.

CYCLAMEN

Close-up of the bud

The showy form of cyclamen, which resembles shooting stars, can be best expressed with *washi* paper. See page 108 for instructions.

Backside view of the blossom, showing how the calyx is attached

DEFINITION OF ORIGAMI SYMBOLS

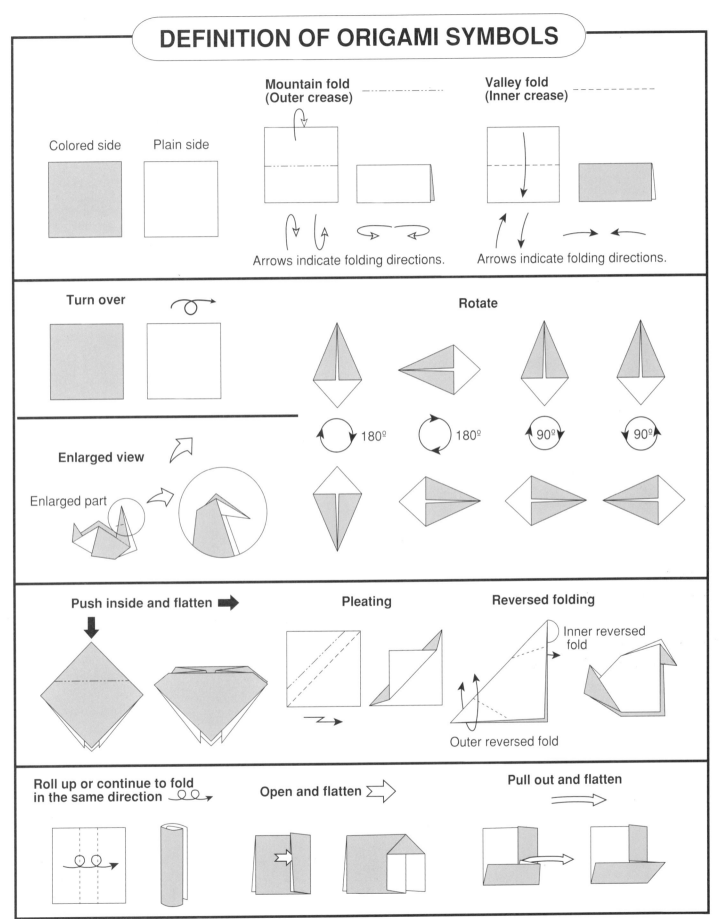

Colored side

Plain side

Mountain fold (Outer crease)

Arrows indicate folding directions.

Valley fold (Inner crease)

Arrows indicate folding directions.

Turn over

Rotate

180° 180° 90° 90°

Enlarged view

Enlarged part

Push inside and flatten

Pleating

Reversed folding

Inner reversed fold

Outer reversed fold

Roll up or continue to fold in the same direction

Open and flatten

Pull out and flatten

BASIC SQUARE

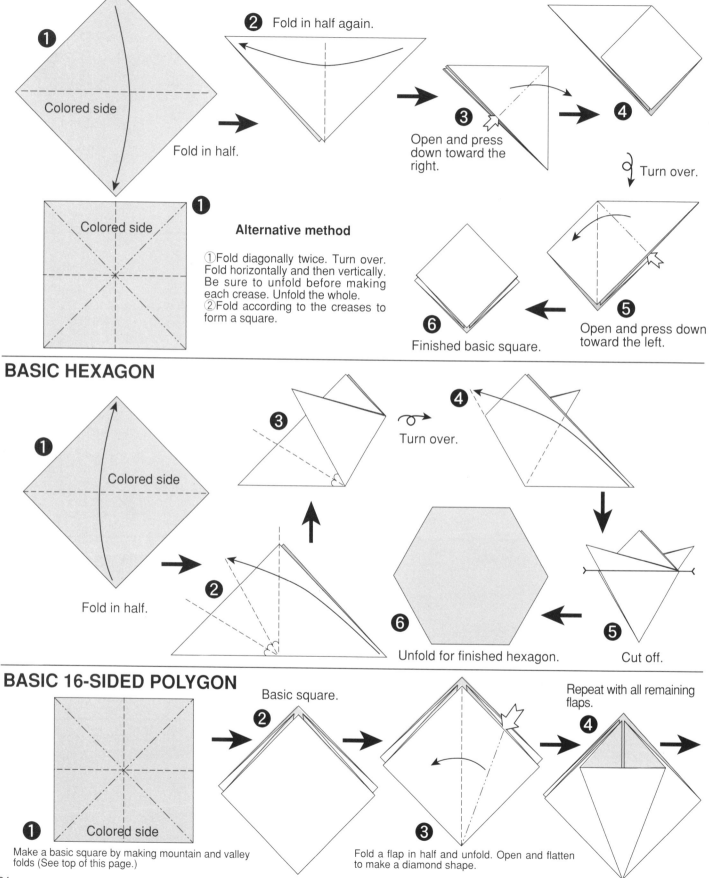

① Colored side
Fold in half.

② Fold in half again.

③ Open and press down toward the right.

④

Turn over.

⑤ Open and press down toward the left.

⑥ Finished basic square.

① Colored side

Alternative method

①Fold diagonally twice. Turn over. Fold horizontally and then vertically. Be sure to unfold before making each crease. Unfold the whole.
②Fold according to the creases to form a square.

BASIC HEXAGON

① Colored side

Fold in half.

②

③

Turn over.

④

⑤ Cut off.

⑥ Unfold for finished hexagon.

BASIC 16-SIDED POLYGON

① Colored side

Make a basic square by making mountain and valley folds (See top of this page.)

Basic square.

②

③ Fold a flap in half and unfold. Open and flatten to make a diamond shape.

Repeat with all remaining flaps.

④

BASIC PENTAGON

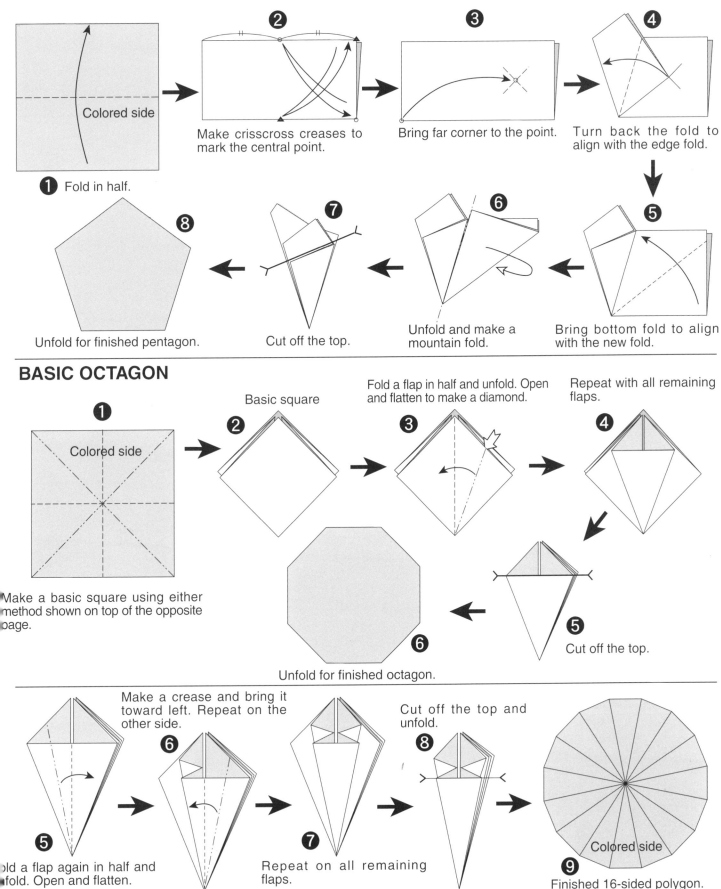

❶ Fold in half.

❷ Make crisscross creases to mark the central point.

❸ Bring far corner to the point.

❹ Turn back the fold to align with the edge fold.

❺ Bring bottom fold to align with the new fold.

❻ Unfold and make a mountain fold.

❼ Cut off the top.

❽ Unfold for finished pentagon.

BASIC OCTAGON

❶ Make a basic square using either method shown on top of the opposite page.

❷ Basic square

❸ Fold a flap in half and unfold. Open and flatten to make a diamond.

❹ Repeat with all remaining flaps.

❺ Cut off the top.

❻ Unfold for finished octagon.

❺ Fold a flap again in half and unfold. Open and flatten.

❻ Make a crease and bring it toward left. Repeat on the other side.

❼ Repeat on all remaining flaps.

❽ Cut off the top and unfold.

❾ Finished 16-sided polygon.

PANSY (Shown on page 8)

Paper materials needed for each blossom
Blossom : 1 sheet (6", solid or shaded color)
Leaves : *Washi* paper (green)
Other materials
Wrapped floral wire: #20 for stems, #24 for leaves

⅛" thick wrapped floral wire
Floral tape (both deep green and yellow)
Alcohol-based marker

See page 110 for LEAF PATTERNS.

"Sheet" means a square sheet of origami or similar paper.

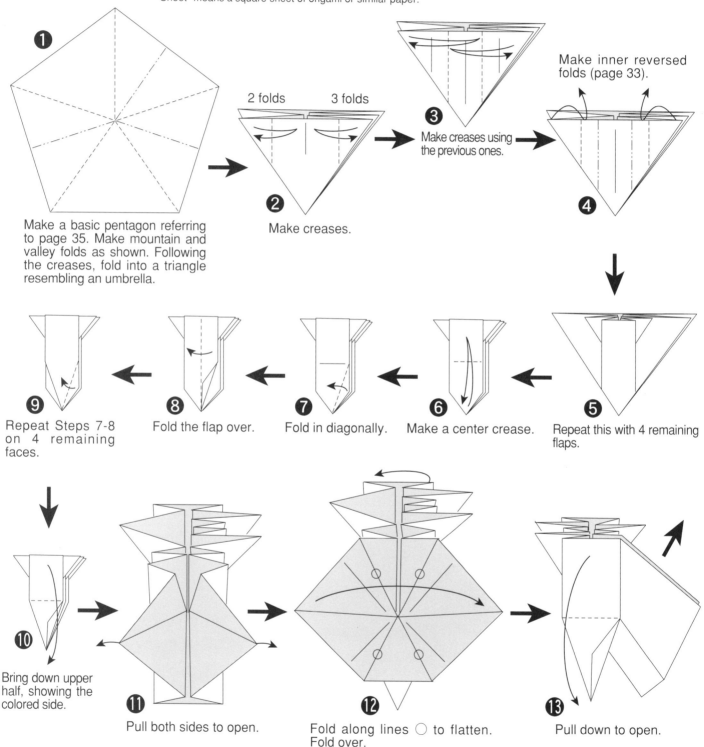

1 Make a basic pentagon referring to page 35. Make mountain and valley folds as shown. Following the creases, fold into a triangle resembling an umbrella.

2 Make creases. 2 folds 3 folds

3 Make creases using the previous ones.

4 Make inner reversed folds (page 33).

5 Repeat this with 4 remaining flaps.

6 Make a center crease.

7 Fold in diagonally.

8 Fold the flap over.

9 Repeat Steps 7-8 on 4 remaining faces.

10 Bring down upper half, showing the colored side.

11 Pull both sides to open.

12 Fold along lines ○ to flatten. Fold over.

13 Pull down to open.

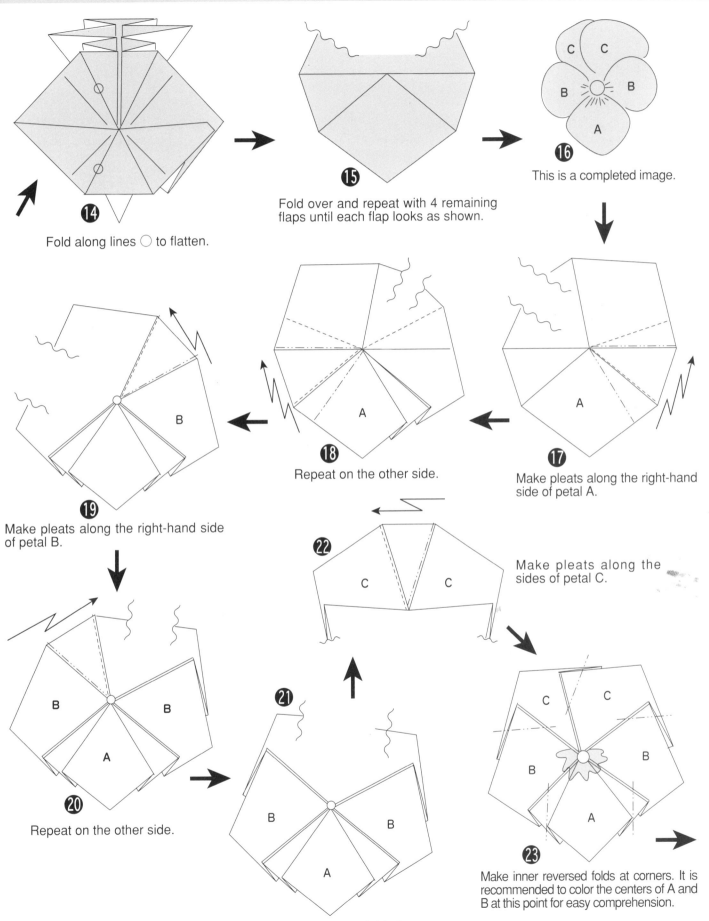

⑭ Fold along lines ○ to flatten.

⑮ Fold over and repeat with 4 remaining flaps until each flap looks as shown.

⑯ This is a completed image.

⑰ Make pleats along the right-hand side of petal A.

⑱ Repeat on the other side.

⑲ Make pleats along the right-hand side of petal B.

⑳ Repeat on the other side.

㉑ Three petals are folded.

㉒ Make pleats along the sides of petal C.

㉓ Make inner reversed folds at corners. It is recommended to color the centers of A and B at this point for easy comprehension.

37

PANSY

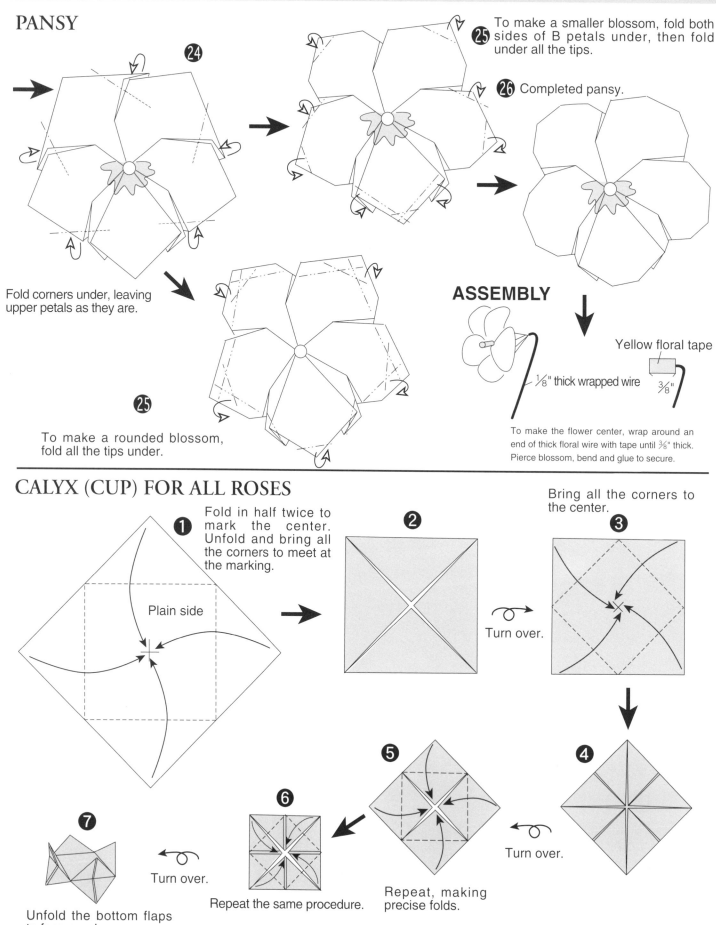

24 Fold corners under, leaving upper petals as they are.

25 To make a rounded blossom, fold all the tips under.

25 To make a smaller blossom, fold both sides of B petals under, then fold under all the tips.

26 Completed pansy.

ASSEMBLY

Yellow floral tape

⅛" thick wrapped wire ⅜"

To make the flower center, wrap around an end of thick floral wire with tape until ⅜" thick. Pierce blossom, bend and glue to secure.

CALYX (CUP) FOR ALL ROSES

1 Fold in half twice to mark the center. Unfold and bring all the corners to meet at the marking.

Plain side

2

3 Bring all the corners to the center.

Turn over.

4

Turn over.

5 Repeat, making precise folds.

6 Repeat the same procedure.

7 Unfold the bottom flaps to form a calyx.

Turn over.

ROSE #1 (Shown on page 2)

Paper materials needed for each blossom and bud

Blossom : 3 sheets (3", 4", and 6", shaded color)
Center : 1 sheet (2¼", shaded color)
Calyx (cup) : 1 sheet (6", green)
Bud : 1 sheet (3", double-sided green)
Leaves : *Washi* paper (green)

Other materials

Wrapped floral wire: #18 for stems, #24 for leaves
Floral tape (deep green)

See page 112 for LEAF PATTERNS.

"Sheet" means a square sheet of origami or similar paper.

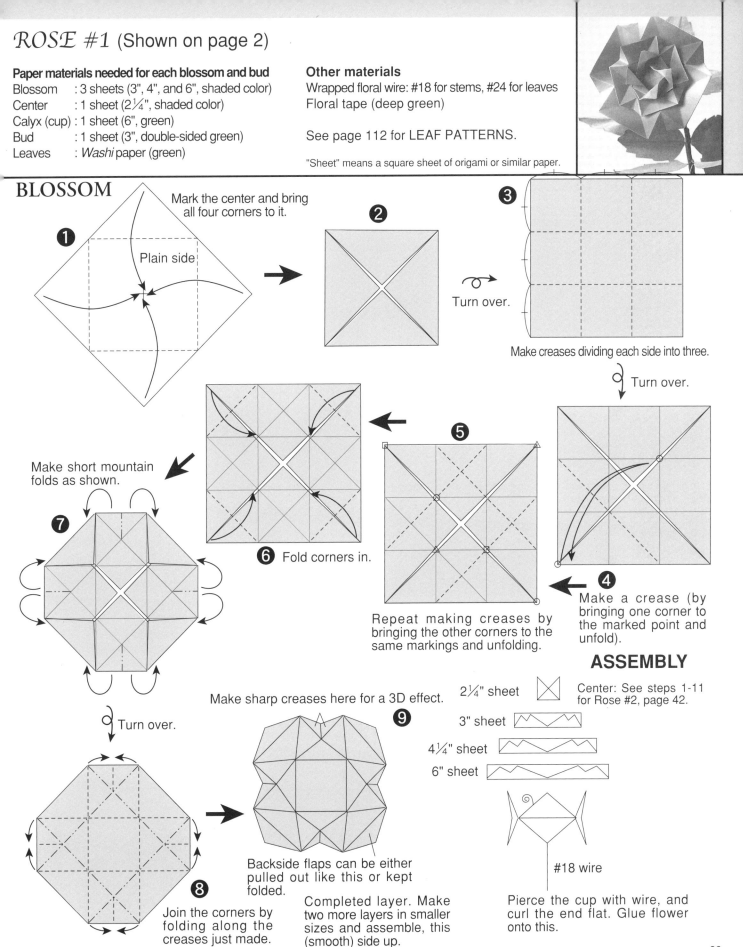

BLOSSOM

❶ Mark the center and bring all four corners to it.

Plain side

❷

Turn over.

❸ Make creases dividing each side into three.

Turn over.

❹ Make a crease (by bringing one corner to the marked point and unfold).

❺ Repeat making creases by bringing the other corners to the same markings and unfolding.

❻ Fold corners in.

Make short mountain folds as shown.

❼

Turn over.

❽ Join the corners by folding along the creases just made.

Make sharp creases here for a 3D effect.

❾

Backside flaps can be either pulled out like this or kept folded.

Completed layer. Make two more layers in smaller sizes and assemble, this (smooth) side up.

ASSEMBLY

Center: See steps 1-11 for Rose #2, page 42.

2¼" sheet

3" sheet

4¼" sheet

6" sheet

#18 wire

Pierce the cup with wire, and curl the end flat. Glue flower onto this.

ROSE #3 (Shown on page 3)

Paper materials needed for each blossom

Blossom : 5 sheets (3¼", 3¾", 4¼", 5" and 6",
                  solid or shaded soft type *washi*)
Calyx(cup) : 1 sheet (6", green)
Leaves : *Washi* paper (green)

Other materials

Wrapped floral wire: #18 for stems , #24 for leaves
Floral tape (deep green)

See page 110 for LEAF PATTERNS.

BLOSSOM

"Sheet" means a square sheet of origami or similar paper.

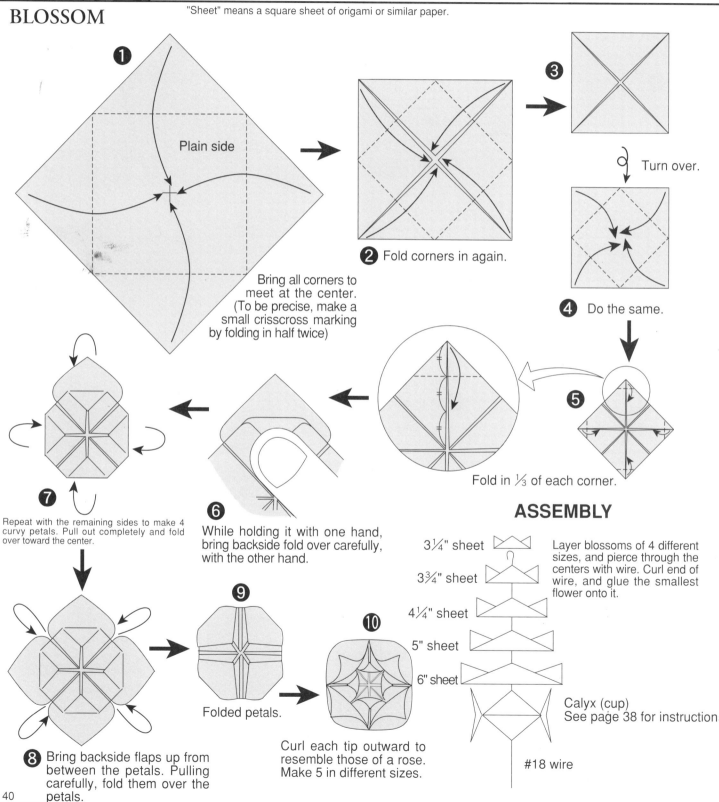

❶ Plain side

Bring all corners to meet at the center. (To be precise, make a small crisscross marking by folding in half twice)

❷ Fold corners in again.

❸

Turn over.

❹ Do the same.

❺ Fold in ⅓ of each corner.

❻ While holding it with one hand, bring backside fold over carefully, with the other hand.

❼ Repeat with the remaining sides to make 4 curvy petals. Pull out completely and fold over toward the center.

❽ Bring backside flaps up from between the petals. Pulling carefully, fold them over the petals.

❾ Folded petals.

❿ Curl each tip outward to resemble those of a rose. Make 5 in different sizes.

ASSEMBLY

3¼" sheet
3¾" sheet
4¼" sheet
5" sheet
6" sheet

Layer blossoms of 4 different sizes, and pierce through the centers with wire. Curl end of wire, and glue the smallest flower onto it.

Calyx (cup)
See page 38 for instruction

#18 wire

40

ROSEBUD (Use double-sided origami of green shades.)

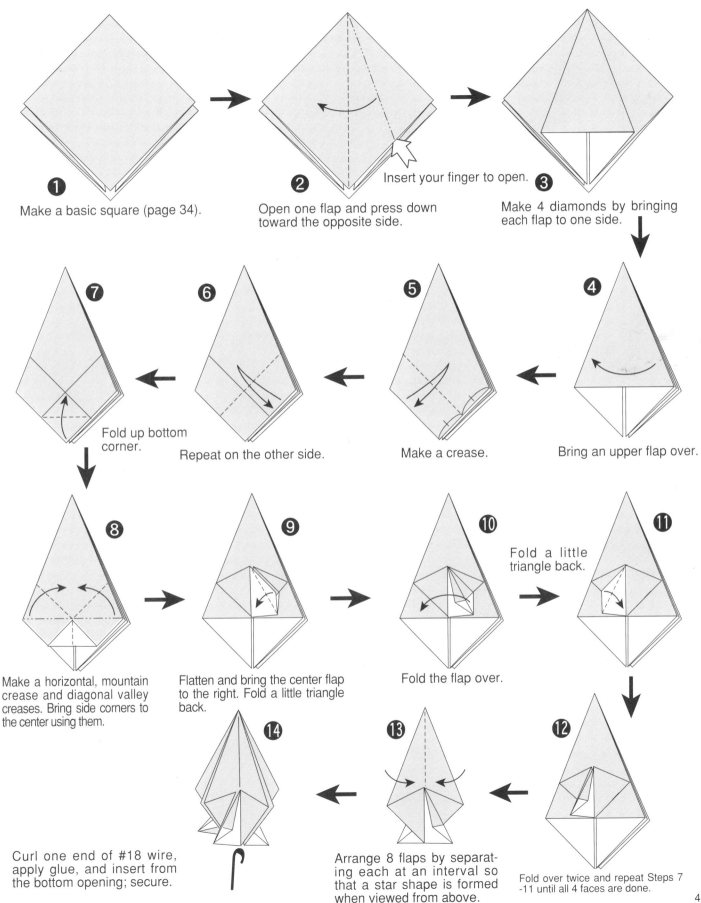

① Make a basic square (page 34).

② Open one flap and press down toward the opposite side.

Insert your finger to open.

③ Make 4 diamonds by bringing each flap to one side.

④ Bring an upper flap over.

⑤ Make a crease.

⑥ Repeat on the other side.

⑦ Fold up bottom corner.

⑧ Make a horizontal, mountain crease and diagonal valley creases. Bring side corners to the center using them.

⑨ Flatten and bring the center flap to the right. Fold a little triangle back.

⑩ Fold the flap over.

⑪ Fold a little triangle back.

⑫ Fold over twice and repeat Steps 7 -11 until all 4 faces are done.

⑬ Arrange 8 flaps by separating each at an interval so that a star shape is formed when viewed from above.

⑭ Curl one end of #18 wire, apply glue, and insert from the bottom opening; secure.

ROSE #2 (Shown on page 2)

Paper materials needed for each blossom and bud
Blossom : 2 sheets (4¼" and 5, shaded color)
              2 sheets (6", shaded color)
Center : 1 sheet (3", shaded color)
Calyx(cup) : 1 sheet (6", green)
Bud : 1 sheet (3", double-sided green)

Leaves : *Washi* paper (green)
Other materials
Wrapped floral wire : #18 for stems , #24 for leaves
Floral tape (deep green)

See page 110 for LEAF PATTERNS.

BLOSSOM

"Sheet" means a square sheet of origami or similar paper.

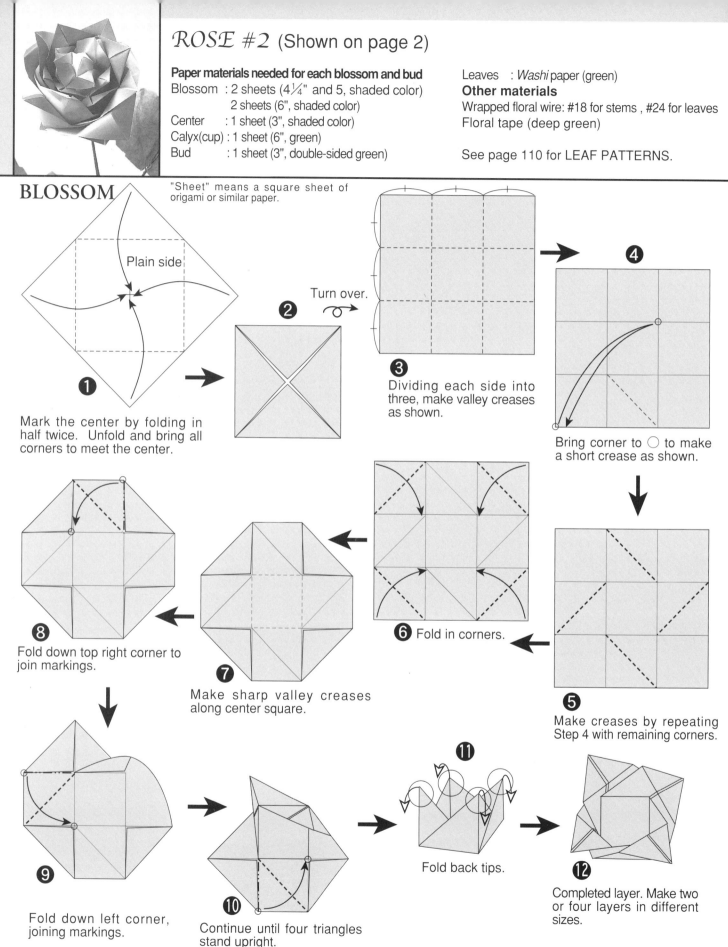

Plain side

❶ Mark the center by folding in half twice. Unfold and bring all corners to meet the center.

❷ Turn over.

❸ Dividing each side into three, make valley creases as shown.

❹ Bring corner to ○ to make a short crease as shown.

❺ Make creases by repeating Step 4 with remaining corners.

❻ Fold in corners.

❼ Make sharp valley creases along center square.

❽ Fold down top right corner to join markings.

❾ Fold down left corner, joining markings.

❿ Continue until four triangles stand upright.

⓫ Fold back tips.

⓬ Completed layer. Make two or four layers in different sizes.

42

CENTER OF FLOWER (Use 3" sheet.)

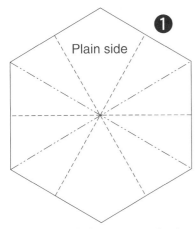

① Plain side

Make a basic hexagon, referring to page 34. Make mountain and valley creases as shown, and fold along them to resemble an umbrella. Flatten.

② Fold down top layer so marking ○ are joined. Spread inside, forming a hexagon again.

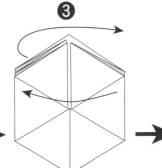

③ Fold the right flap over, and fold the backside flap as well.

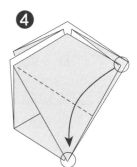

④ Repeat Step 2, and spread open the inside, forming a hexagon.

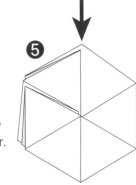

⑤

Turn over.

⑥ Repeat once more, and spread open the inside.

⑦

Rotate.

⑧ Insert your finger into the opening to form a pyramid.

⑨ Bring the side corners to meet at the back.

⑩ Completed center of flower.

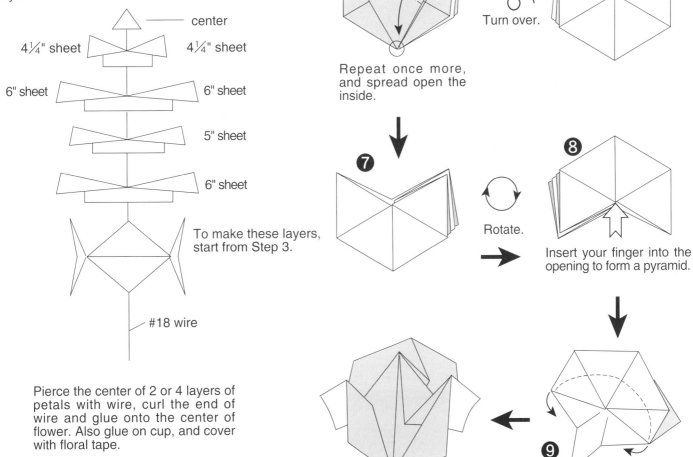

Make 4 layers for a red rose (see page 4), 2 layers for a blue rose.

center

4¼" sheet   4¼" sheet

6" sheet   6" sheet

5" sheet

6" sheet

To make these layers, start from Step 3.

#18 wire

Pierce the center of 2 or 4 layers of petals with wire, curl the end of wire and glue onto the center of flower. Also glue on cup, and cover with floral tape.

ASSEMBLY

HYACINTH (Shown on page 4)

Paper materials needed for each floret
1 sheet (6" , solid color)
Leaves: *Washi* paper (green)
Other materials
Wrapped floral wire: #18 for stems , #24 for leaves
⅛" thick wrapped floral wire (green)

Floral tape (deep green)

See page 110 for LEAF PATTERNS.

"Sheet" means a square sheet of origami or similar paper.

FLORET

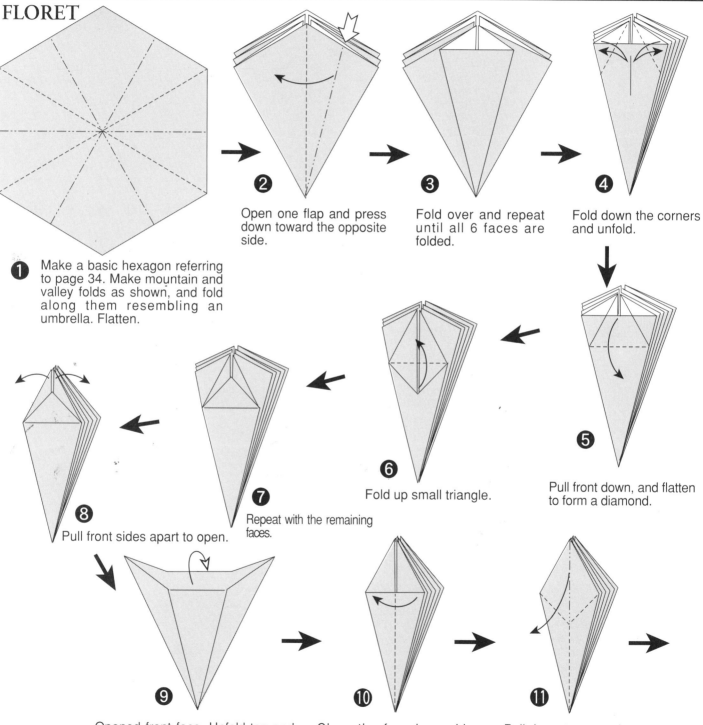

❶ Make a basic hexagon referring to page 34. Make mountain and valley folds as shown, and fold along them resembling an umbrella. Flatten.

❷ Open one flap and press down toward the opposite side.

❸ Fold over and repeat until all 6 faces are folded.

❹ Fold down the corners and unfold.

❺ Pull front down, and flatten to form a diamond.

❻ Fold up small triangle.

❼ Repeat with the remaining faces.

❽ Pull front sides apart to open.

❾ Opened front face. Unfold top and fold back.

❿ Close the face by making a valley fold. Fold one flap over.

⓫ Pull down top to make an inner reversed fold by bringing the right-side flap to left.

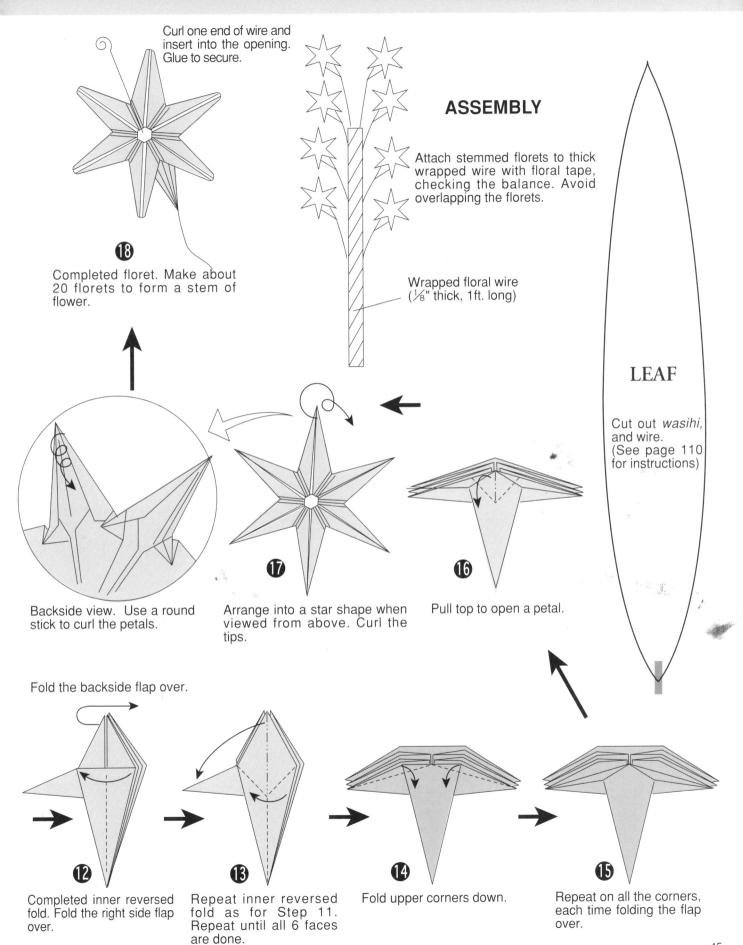

Curl one end of wire and insert into the opening. Glue to secure.

ASSEMBLY

Attach stemmed florets to thick wrapped wire with floral tape, checking the balance. Avoid overlapping the florets.

Wrapped floral wire (⅛" thick, 1ft. long)

⑱ Completed floret. Make about 20 florets to form a stem of flower.

LEAF

Cut out *wasihi*, and wire. (See page 110 for instructions)

Backside view. Use a round stick to curl the petals.

⑰ Arrange into a star shape when viewed from above. Curl the tips.

⑯ Pull top to open a petal.

Fold the backside flap over.

⑫ Completed inner reversed fold. Fold the right side flap over.

⑬ Repeat inner reversed fold as for Step 11. Repeat until all 6 faces are done.

⑭ Fold upper corners down.

⑮ Repeat on all the corners, each time folding the flap over.

45

CARNATION (Shown on page 7)

Paper materials needed for each floret and bud

Blossom : 2-3 sheets (6", *washi* tissue)
Calyx (cup) : 1 sheet (3", pale green)
Bud : 1 sheet (3", red or pink *washi* paper)
: 1 sheet (3", green *washi* paper)

"Sheet" means a square sheet of origami or similar paper.

Other materials

Wrapped floral wire: #20 for stems, #24 for leaves

Floral tape (green)

BLOSSOM

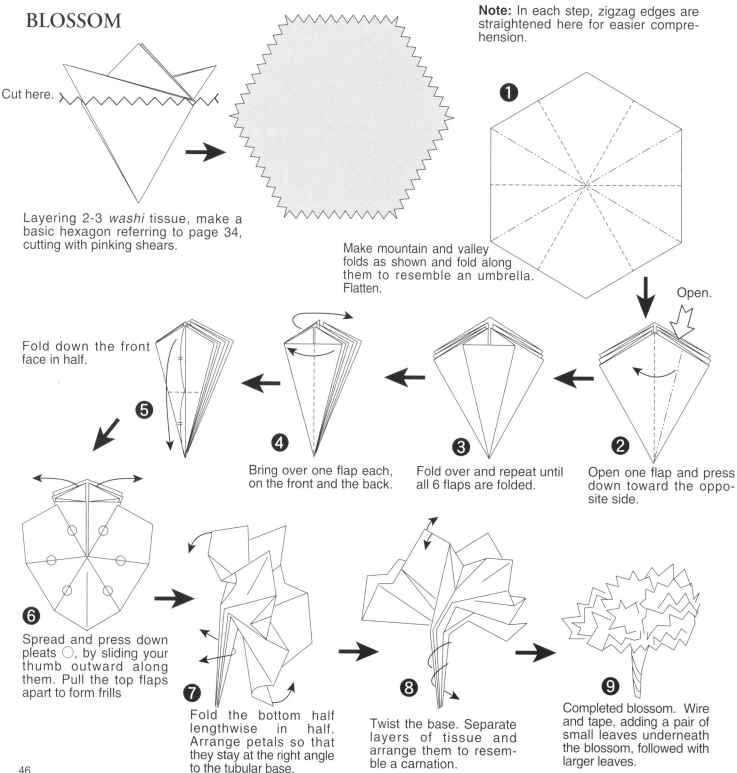

Cut here.

Layering 2-3 *washi* tissue, make a basic hexagon referring to page 34, cutting with pinking shears.

Note: In each step, zigzag edges are straightened here for easier comprehension.

❶ Make mountain and valley folds as shown and fold along them to resemble an umbrella. Flatten.

Open.

❷ Open one flap and press down toward the opposite side.

❸ Fold over and repeat until all 6 flaps are folded.

❹ Bring over one flap each, on the front and the back.

Fold down the front face in half.

❺

❻ Spread and press down pleats ○, by sliding your thumb outward along them. Pull the top flaps apart to form frills

❼ Fold the bottom half lengthwise in half. Arrange petals so that they stay at the right angle to the tubular base.

❽ Twist the base. Separate layers of tissue and arrange them to resemble a carnation.

❾ Completed blossom. Wire and tape, adding a pair of small leaves underneath the blossom, followed with larger leaves.

46

BUD / CALYX (CUP)

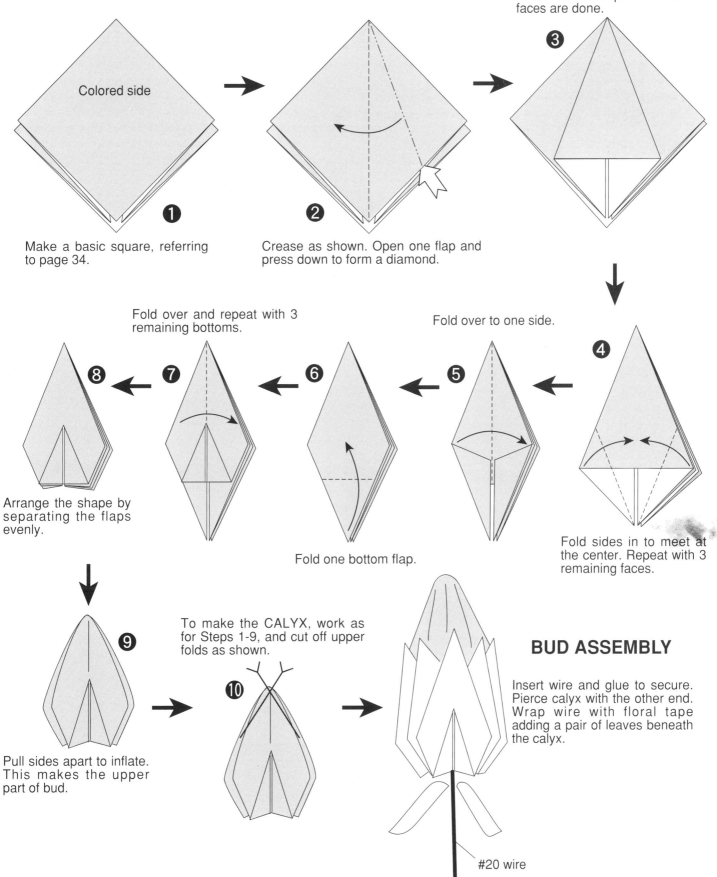

1 Make a basic square, referring to page 34.

2 Crease as shown. Open one flap and press down to form a diamond.

Fold over and repeat until all 4 faces are done.

3

Fold sides in to meet at the center. Repeat with 3 remaining faces.

4

Fold over to one side.

5

6 Fold one bottom flap.

Fold over and repeat with 3 remaining bottoms.

7

8 Arrange the shape by separating the flaps evenly.

9 Pull sides apart to inflate. This makes the upper part of bud.

To make the CALYX, work as for Steps 1-9, and cut off upper folds as shown.

10

BUD ASSEMBLY

Insert wire and glue to secure. Pierce calyx with the other end. Wrap wire with floral tape adding a pair of leaves beneath the calyx.

#20 wire

47

$\mathcal{VIOLET}$ (Shown on page 8)

Paper materials needed for each floret and bud
Blossom : 1 sheet (5", violet)
Calyx (cup) : 1 sheet (3", green)
Bud : 1 sheet (3", violet)
Leaves : *Washi* paper (green)

Other materials
Wrapped floral wire: #24 for both stem and leaves
Floral tape (deep green)
See page 110 for LEAF PATTERNS.

"Sheet" means a square sheet of origami or similar paper.

CALYX (CUP)

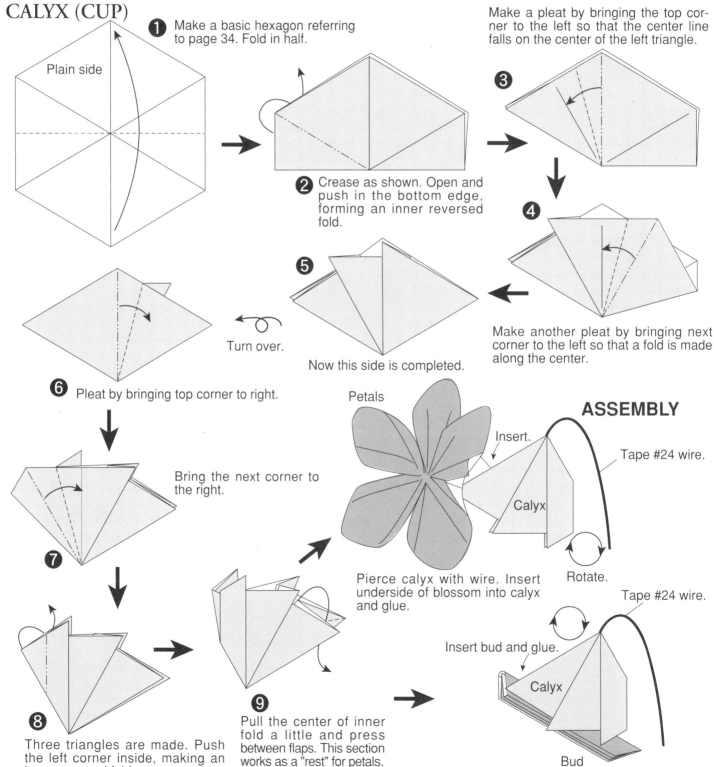

1 Make a basic hexagon referring to page 34. Fold in half.

Plain side

Make a pleat by bringing the top corner to the left so that the center line falls on the center of the left triangle.

3

2 Crease as shown. Open and push in the bottom edge, forming an inner reversed fold.

4

Make another pleat by bringing next corner to the left so that a fold is made along the center.

5 Now this side is completed.

Turn over.

6 Pleat by bringing top corner to right.

Bring the next corner to the right.

7

8 Three triangles are made. Push the left corner inside, making an inner reversed fold.

9 Pull the center of inner fold a little and press between flaps. This section works as a "rest" for petals.

Petals

Pierce calyx with wire. Insert underside of blossom into calyx and glue.

Insert.

Calyx

ASSEMBLY

Tape #24 wire.

Rotate.

Tape #24 wire.

Insert bud and glue.

Calyx

Bud

48

BLOSSOM / BUD

1 Make a basic pentagon, referring to page 35. Make mountain and valley creases as shown, and fold along them resembling an umbrella. Flatten.

Colored side

2 Crease vertically by folding corners to meet at the center.

2 folds   3 folds

3 Crease as shown.

4 Open top and push the side triangles inside so that the corners peak out between vertical folds.

5 Small triangles are peaking out between the mountain folds.

6 Repeat with all the remaining faces.

BLOSSOM

7 Fold down the front in half.

8 Make an inner reversed fold on the side triangles so that the colored side shows. Do the same with remaining flaps, pulling down in each direction.

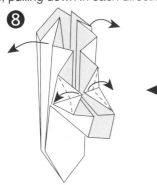

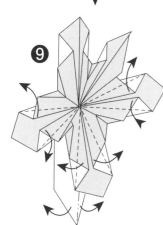

9 Fold back the center folds of petals diagonally. Fold base in half so that the sides meet behind. This opens the petals.

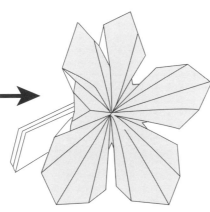

10 Spread 3 lower petals, flattening the center creases, and let the top 2 petals face each other.

BUD

7 Do the same as BLOSSOM from Step 1 through 6. Fold in half.

8 Completed bud.

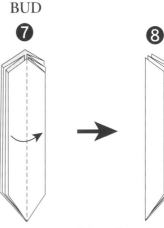

STOCK (Shown on page 5)

Paper materials needed for each floret (cluster type)
Blossom : 2 sheets (3½", solid color)
: 2 sheets (3", solid color)
Center : 1 sheet (3", solid color)

Paper materials needed for each floret, bud, and calyx (branched type)
Blossom : 2 sheets (3" and 2¼", white)
Bud : 1 sheet (2", white)

Calyx (cup) : 1 sheet (2", green)
Leaves : *Washi* paper (green)

Other materials
Wrapped floral wire: #20 for stems, #24 for leaves
⅛" thick wrapped wire (green)
Floral tape (both pale green and deep green)

See page 111 for LEAF PATTERNS

FLORET

"Sheet" means a square sheet of origami or similar paper.

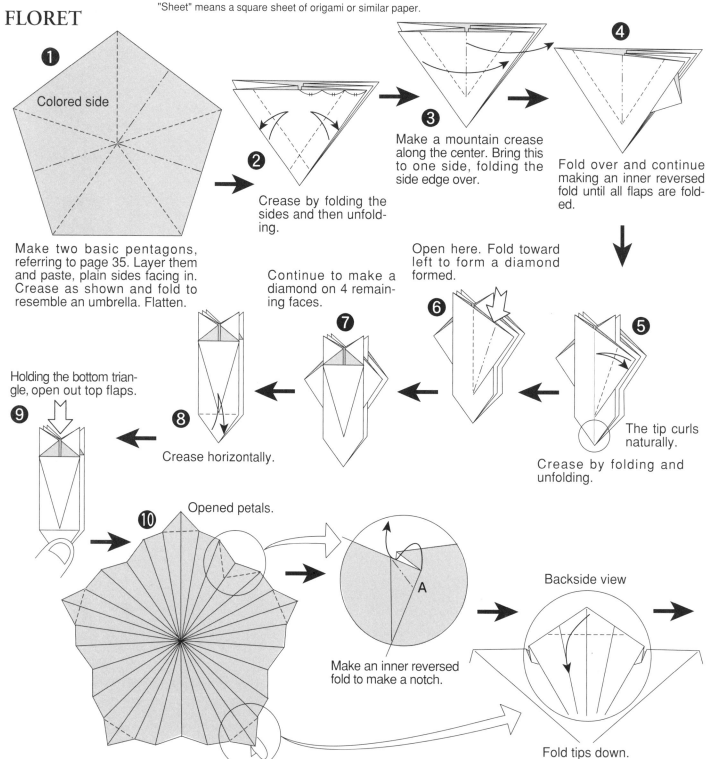

❶ Colored side

Make two basic pentagons, referring to page 35. Layer them and paste, plain sides facing in. Crease as shown and fold to resemble an umbrella. Flatten.

❷ Crease by folding the sides and then unfolding.

❸ Make a mountain crease along the center. Bring this to one side, folding the side edge over.

❹ Fold over and continue making an inner reversed fold until all flaps are folded.

❺ The tip curls naturally.
Crease by folding and unfolding.

❻ Open here. Fold toward left to form a diamond formed.

❼ Continue to make a diamond on 4 remaining faces.

❽ Crease horizontally.

❾ Holding the bottom triangle, open out top flaps.

❿ Opened petals.

Make an inner reversed fold to make a notch.

A

Backside view

Fold tips down.

CENTER OF FLOWER (Use 3" sheet.)

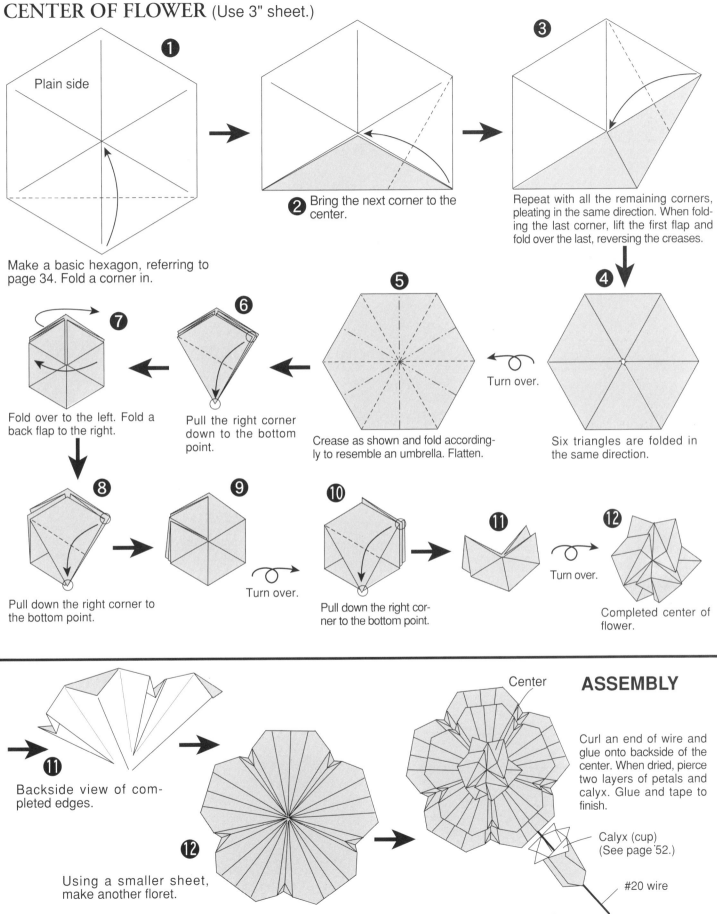

❶ Plain side

Make a basic hexagon, referring to page 34. Fold a corner in.

❷ Bring the next corner to the center.

❸ Repeat with all the remaining corners, pleating in the same direction. When folding the last corner, lift the first flap and fold over the last, reversing the creases.

❹ Turn over. Six triangles are folded in the same direction.

❺ Crease as shown and fold accordingly to resemble an umbrella. Flatten.

❻ Pull the right corner down to the bottom point.

❼ Fold over to the left. Fold a back flap to the right.

❽ Pull down the right corner to the bottom point.

❾ Turn over.

❿ Pull down the right corner to the bottom point.

⓫ Turn over.

⓬ Completed center of flower.

ASSEMBLY

⓫ Backside view of completed edges.

⓬ Using a smaller sheet, make another floret.

Center

Curl an end of wire and glue onto backside of the center. When dried, pierce two layers of petals and calyx. Glue and tape to finish.

Calyx (cup) (See page 52.)

#20 wire

51

CALYX (CUP) FOR STOCK (Use 2" sheet.)

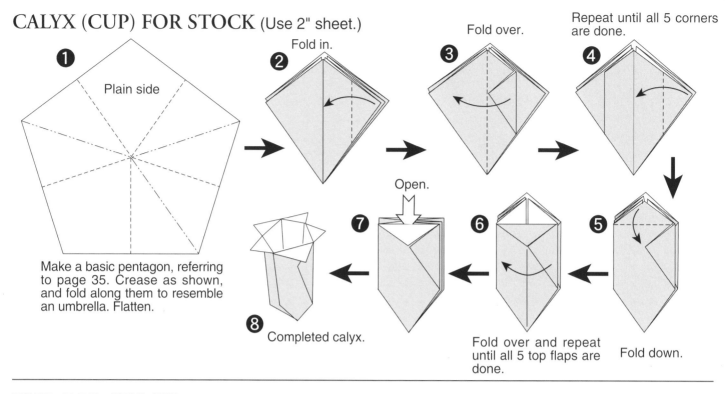

❶ Plain side

Make a basic pentagon, referring to page 35. Crease as shown, and fold along them to resemble an umbrella. Flatten.

❷ Fold in.

❸ Fold over.

❹ Repeat until all 5 corners are done.

❺ Fold down.

❻ Fold over and repeat until all 5 top flaps are done.

❼ Open.

❽ Completed calyx.

BUD FOR STOCK (Use 2" sheet.)

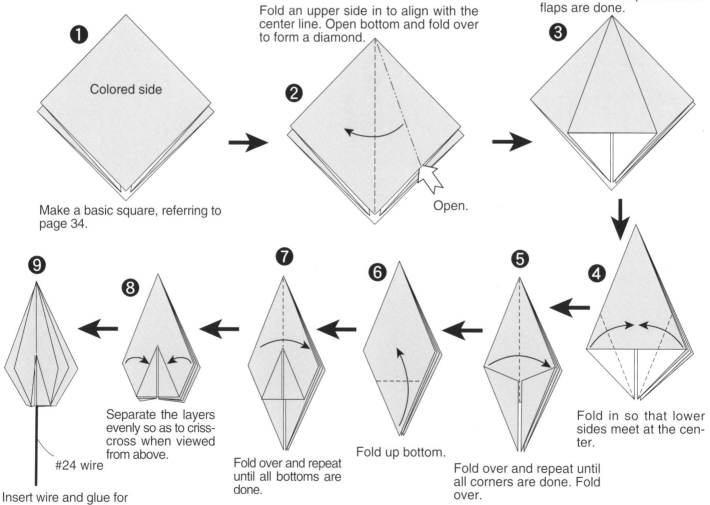

❶ Colored side

Make a basic square, referring to page 34.

❷ Fold an upper side in to align with the center line. Open bottom and fold over to form a diamond. Open.

❸ Fold over and repeat until all flaps are done.

❹ Fold in so that lower sides meet at the center.

❺ Fold over and repeat until all corners are done. Fold over.

❻ Fold up bottom.

❼ Fold over and repeat until all bottoms are done.

❽ Separate the layers evenly so as to criss-cross when viewed from above.

❾ #24 wire

Insert wire and glue for completed bud.

52

TULIP (Shown on page 6)

Paper materials needed for each blossom
1 sheet (6", white, colored on both sides before folding)
Leaves : *Washi* paper (green)
Other materials
#20 wrapped floral wire for leaves
⅛" thick wrapped wire (green)

Floral tape (green)
Alcohol-based markers

See page 112 for LEAF PATTERNS.

"Sheet" means a square sheet of origami or similar paper.

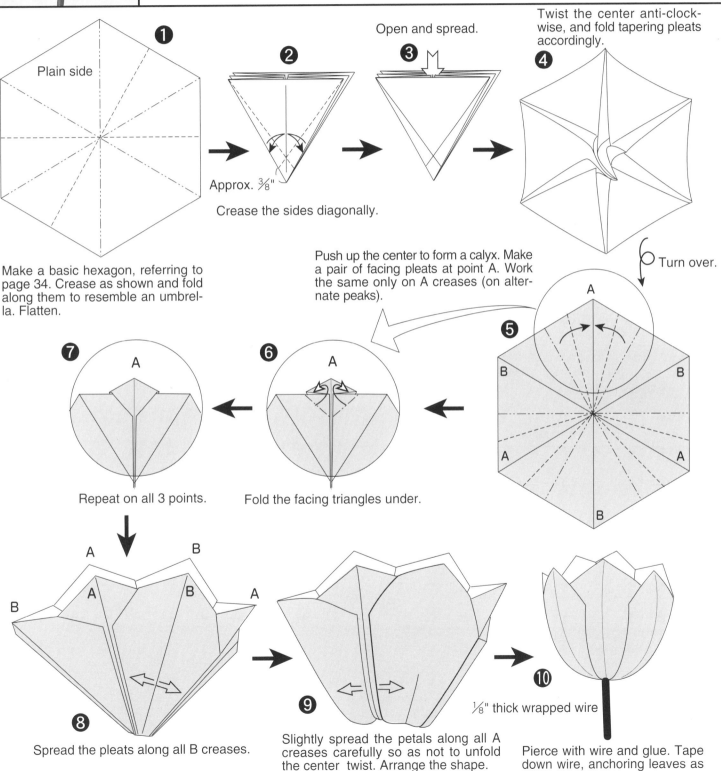

① Plain side

Make a basic hexagon, referring to page 34. Crease as shown and fold along them to resemble an umbrella. Flatten.

② Approx. ⅜"
Crease the sides diagonally.

③ Open and spread.

④ Twist the center anti-clockwise, and fold tapering pleats accordingly.

Turn over.

⑤ Push up the center to form a calyx. Make a pair of facing pleats at point A. Work the same only on A creases (on alternate peaks).

⑥ A
Fold the facing triangles under.

⑦ A
Repeat on all 3 points.

⑧ Spread the pleats along all B creases.

⑨ Slightly spread the petals along all A creases carefully so as not to unfold the center twist. Arrange the shape.

⑩ ⅛" thick wrapped wire
Pierce with wire and glue. Tape down wire, anchoring leaves as you go.

53

Paper materials needed for each blossom
1 sheet (6", yellow or rose)
Leaves : *Washi* paper (green)
Other materials
Wrapped floral wire: #24 for leaves
⅛" thick wrapped wire (green)

Floral tape (both green and yellow)

See page 56 for LEAF PATTERN.

"Sheet" means a square sheet of origami or similar paper.

NARCISSUS #1

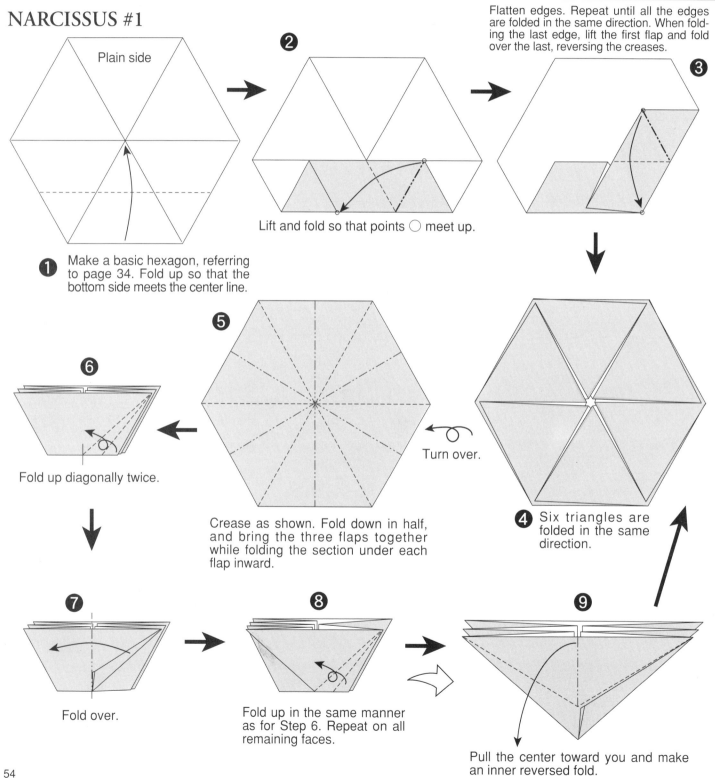

Plain side

❶ Make a basic hexagon, referring to page 34. Fold up so that the bottom side meets the center line.

❷ Lift and fold so that points ○ meet up.

Flatten edges. Repeat until all the edges are folded in the same direction. When folding the last edge, lift the first flap and fold over the last, reversing the creases.

❸

❹ Six triangles are folded in the same direction.

Turn over.

❺ Crease as shown. Fold down in half, and bring the three flaps together while folding the section under each flap inward.

❻ Fold up diagonally twice.

❼ Fold over.

❽ Fold up in the same manner as for Step 6. Repeat on all remaining faces.

❾ Pull the center toward you and make an inner reversed fold.

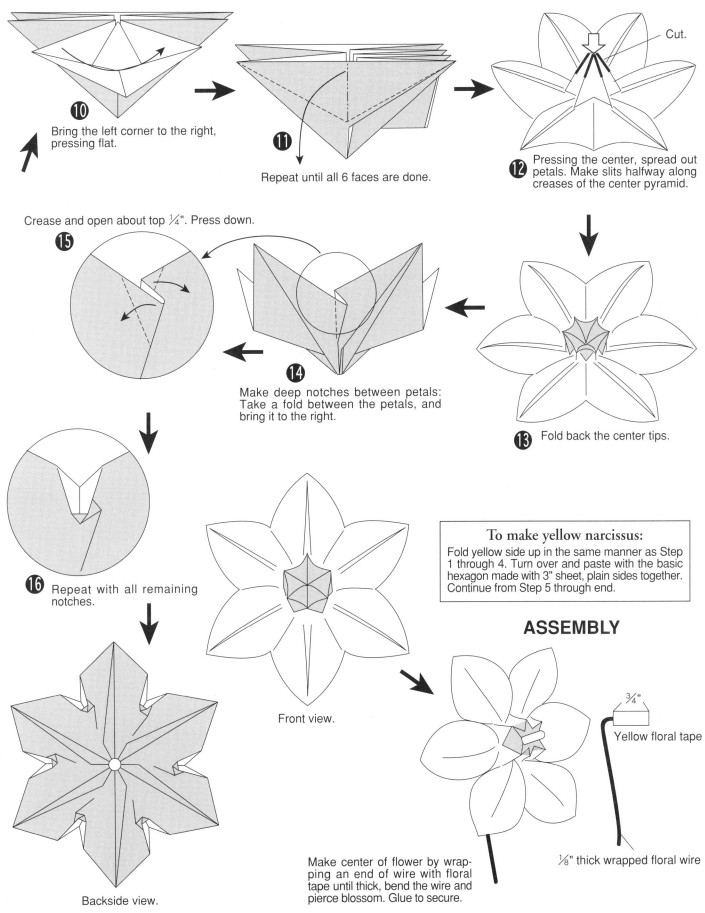

⑩ Bring the left corner to the right, pressing flat.

Repeat until all 6 faces are done.

⑫ Pressing the center, spread out petals. Make slits halfway along creases of the center pyramid.

Cut.

⑬ Fold back the center tips.

Crease and open about top ¼". Press down.

⑮

⑭ Make deep notches between petals: Take a fold between the petals, and bring it to the right.

⑯ Repeat with all remaining notches.

Front view.

Backside view.

To make yellow narcissus:
Fold yellow side up in the same manner as Step 1 through 4. Turn over and paste with the basic hexagon made with 3" sheet, plain sides together. Continue from Step 5 through end.

ASSEMBLY

¾"

Yellow floral tape

⅛" thick wrapped floral wire

Make center of flower by wrapping an end of wire with floral tape until thick, bend the wire and pierce blossom. Glue to secure.

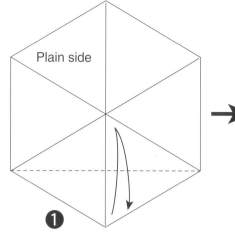

① Make a basic hexagon, referring to page 34. Fold up to the center and unfold.

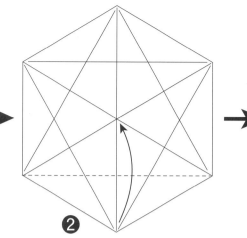

② Repeat with 5 remaining corners to crease. Fold up bottom corner again.

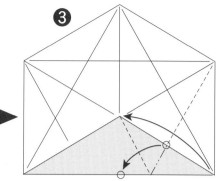

③ Join points ○ together and flatten edges.

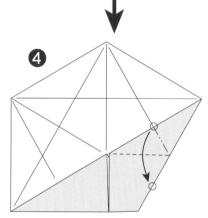

④ Join points ○ together and flatten edges. Repeat until all edges are folded in the same direction.

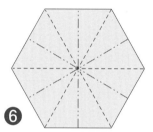

⑥ Crease as shown. Turn over and fold accordingly, pulling out flaps.

Turn over.

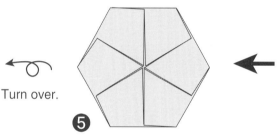

⑤ When folding the last edge, lift the first flap and fold over the last, reversing creases so that each fold faces the same direction.

⑦ Crease as shown by bringing bottoms to the center crease.

⑧ Fold in twice.

⑨ Fold over. Repeat with all 3 remaining side corners.

⑩ Holding at side ○, loosen top.

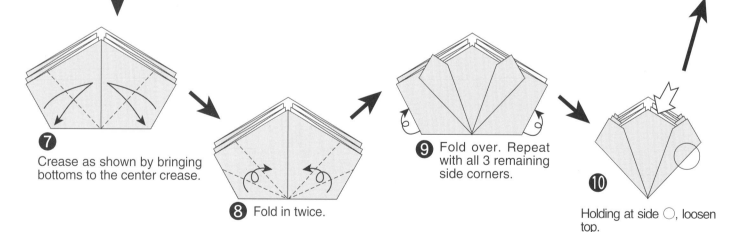

LEAF for both #1 and #2
Cut out *washi*, and wire. (See page 110 for instructions)

A

B

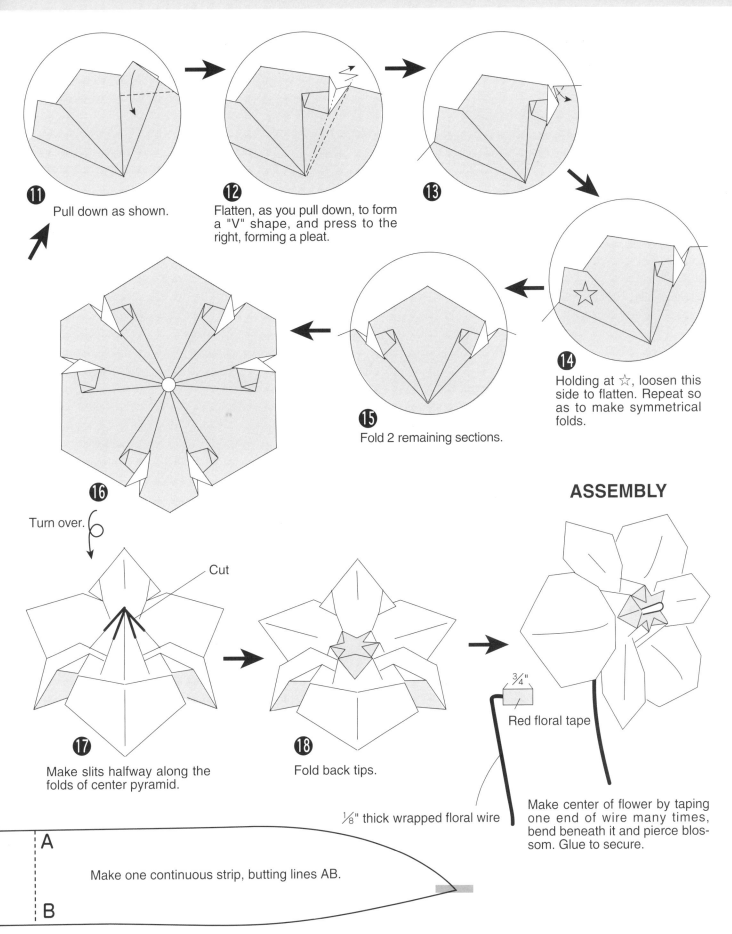

⑪ Pull down as shown.

⑫ Flatten, as you pull down, to form a "V" shape, and press to the right, forming a pleat.

⑬

⑭ Holding at ☆, loosen this side to flatten. Repeat so as to make symmetrical folds.

⑮ Fold 2 remaining sections.

⑯ Turn over.

ASSEMBLY

Cut

⑰ Make slits halfway along the folds of center pyramid.

⑱ Fold back tips.

⅛" thick wrapped floral wire

3/4"

Red floral tape

Make center of flower by taping one end of wire many times, bend beneath it and pierce blossom. Glue to secure.

A

B

Make one continuous strip, butting lines AB.

DOKUDAMI (Shown on page 11)

Paper materials needed for each blossom and stipule

Blossom : 1 sheet (3½", white)
: 1 sheet (2¼", green)
Stipule : 1 sheet (2", shaded green)
Leaves : *Washi* paper (green)

Other materials

Wrapped floral wire: #18 for stems and #24 for leaves
Floral tape (deep green)

"Sheet" means a square sheet of origami or similar paper.

BLOSSOM

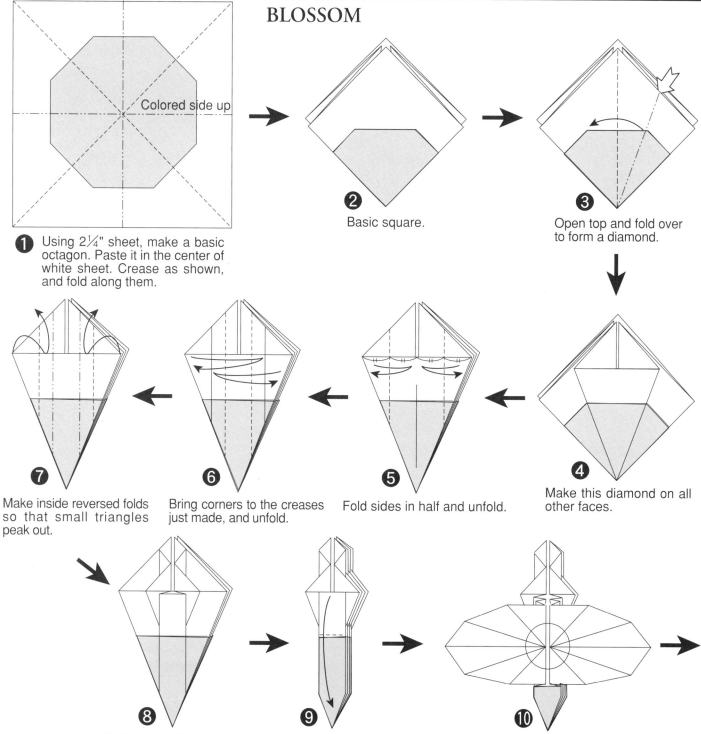

❶ Using 2¼" sheet, make a basic octagon. Paste it in the center of white sheet. Crease as shown, and fold along them.

Colored side up

❷ Basic square.

❸ Open top and fold over to form a diamond.

❹ Make this diamond on all other faces.

❺ Fold sides in half and unfold.

❻ Bring corners to the creases just made, and unfold.

❼ Make inside reversed folds so that small triangles peak out.

❽ Flatten tops. Repeat with all other diamonds.

❾ Pull the front down and flatten.

❿ Holding at the center, spread out the pleats.

STIPULE

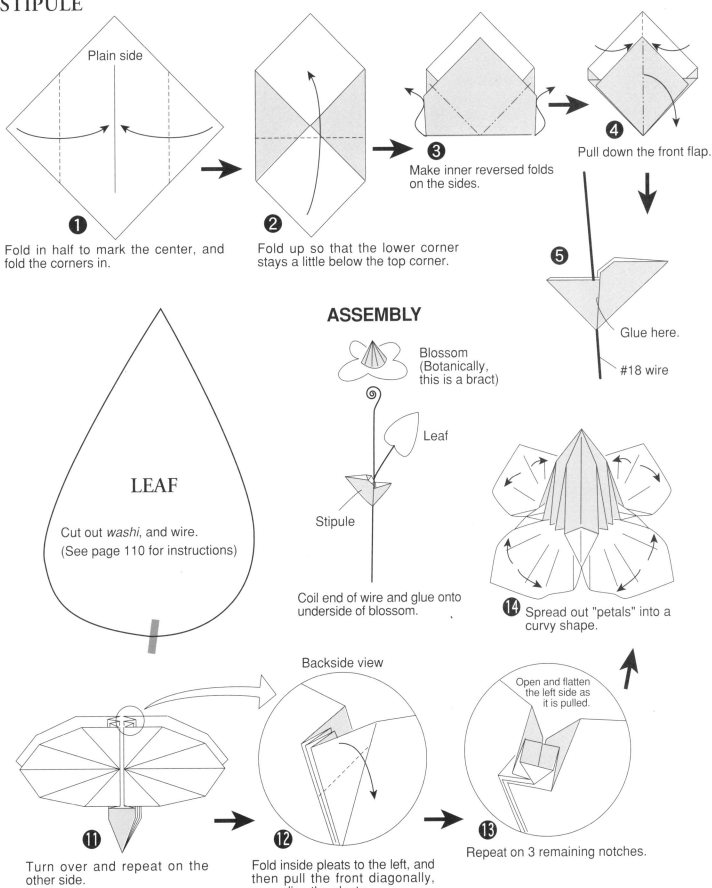

① Plain side — Fold in half to mark the center, and fold the corners in.

② Fold up so that the lower corner stays a little below the top corner.

③ Make inner reversed folds on the sides.

④ Pull down the front flap.

⑤ Glue here.
#18 wire

LEAF

Cut out *washi*, and wire.
(See page 110 for instructions)

ASSEMBLY

Blossom
(Botanically, this is a bract)

Leaf

Stipule

Coil end of wire and glue onto underside of blossom.

⑭ Spread out "petals" into a curvy shape.

⑪ Turn over and repeat on the other side.

Backside view

⑫ Fold inside pleats to the left, and then pull the front diagonally, spreading the pleats.

⑬ Open and flatten the left side as it is pulled.
Repeat on 3 remaining notches.

CINERARIA (Shown on page 12)

Paper materials needed for each blossom
1 sheet (6", solid color or white)
Leaves : *Washi* paper (green)
Other materials
Wrapped floral wire: #20 for flowers, #24 for leaves
⅛" thick wrapped wire (green)

Green floral tapes
Alcohol-based markers

See page 111 for LEAF PATTERNS.

"Sheet" means a square sheet of origami or similar paper.

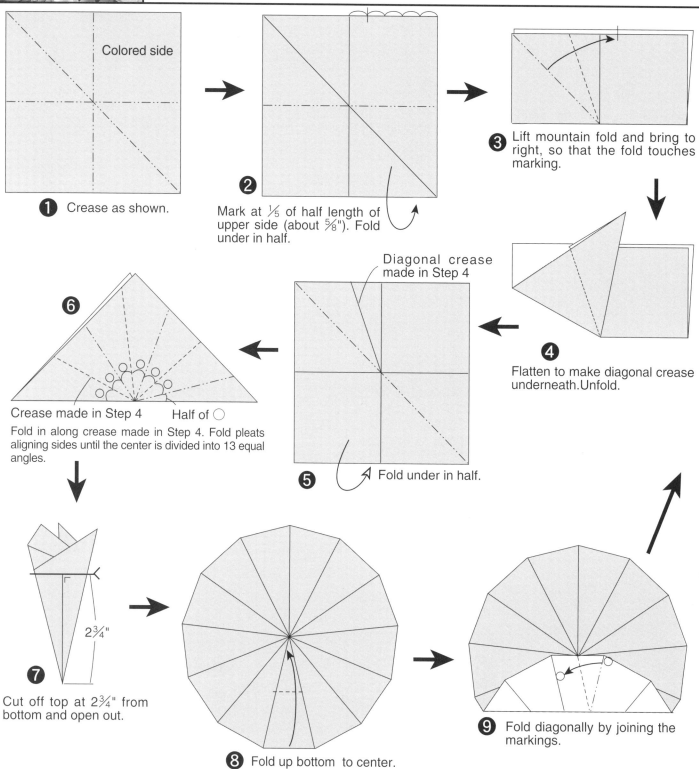

❶ Crease as shown.

Colored side

❷ Mark at ⅕ of half length of upper side (about ⅝"). Fold under in half.

❸ Lift mountain fold and bring to right, so that the fold touches marking.

❹ Flatten to make diagonal crease underneath. Unfold.

Diagonal crease made in Step 4

❺ Fold under in half.

❻
Crease made in Step 4   Half of ○
Fold in along crease made in Step 4. Fold pleats aligning sides until the center is divided into 13 equal angles.

❼ Cut off top at 2¾" from bottom and open out.

2¾"

❽ Fold up bottom to center.

❾ Fold diagonally by joining the markings.

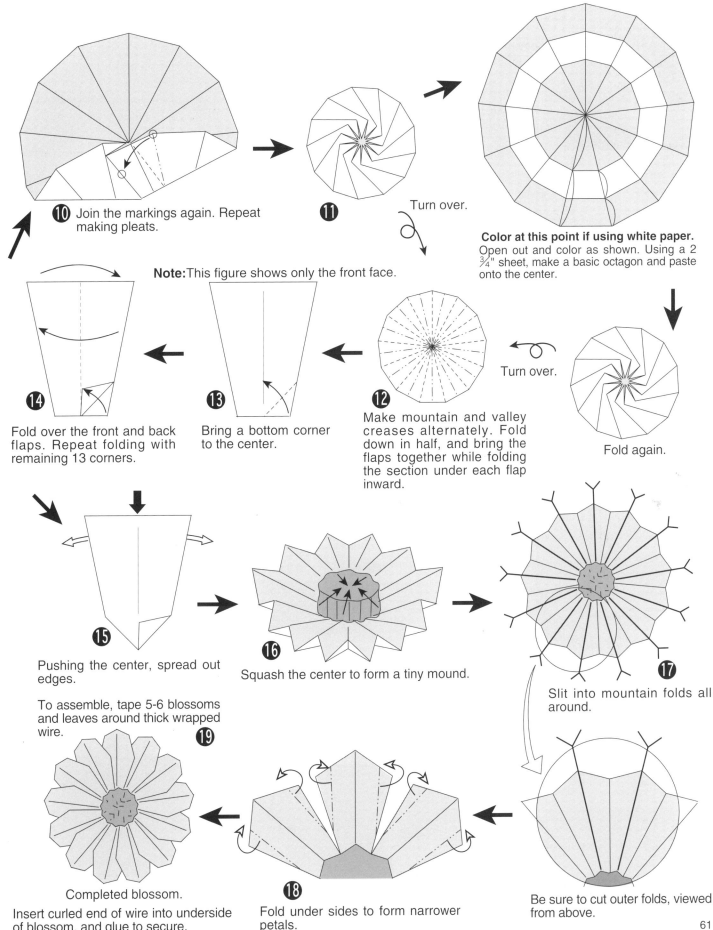

⑩ Join the markings again. Repeat making pleats.

⑪ Turn over.

Color at this point if using white paper.
Open out and color as shown. Using a 2 ¾" sheet, make a basic octagon and paste onto the center.

Note: This figure shows only the front face.

⑭ Fold over the front and back flaps. Repeat folding with remaining 13 corners.

⑬ Bring a bottom corner to the center.

⑫ Make mountain and valley creases alternately. Fold down in half, and bring the flaps together while folding the section under each flap inward.

Turn over.

Fold again.

⑮ Pushing the center, spread out edges.

⑯ Squash the center to form a tiny mound.

⑰ Slit into mountain folds all around.

To assemble, tape 5-6 blossoms and leaves around thick wrapped wire. ⑲

⑱ Fold under sides to form narrower petals.

Be sure to cut outer folds, viewed from above.

Completed blossom.
Insert curled end of wire into underside of blossom, and glue to secure.

61

POLYANTHUS PRIMROSE (Shown on page 13)

Paper materials needed for each blossom
Blossom : 1 sheet (4½", solid color)
Center : 1 sheet (2¼", solid color)
Leaves : *Washi* paper (green)
Other materials
Wrapped floral wire: #20 for stems, #24 for leaves

⅛" thick wrapped wire (green)
Floral tape (both pale green and deep green)

"Sheet" means a square sheet of origami or similar paper.

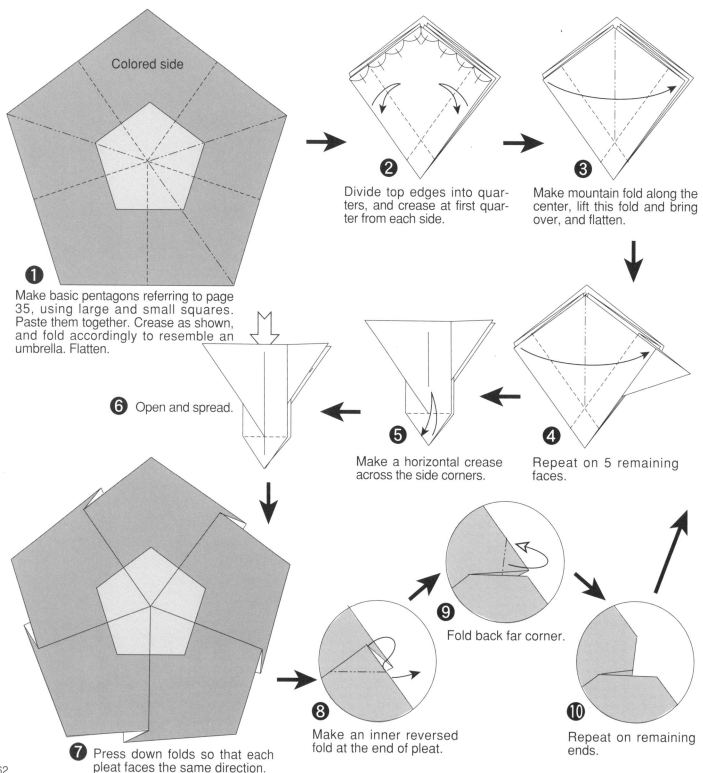

① Make basic pentagons referring to page 35, using large and small squares. Paste them together. Crease as shown, and fold accordingly to resemble an umbrella. Flatten.

② Divide top edges into quarters, and crease at first quarter from each side.

③ Make mountain fold along the center, lift this fold and bring over, and flatten.

④ Repeat on 5 remaining faces.

⑤ Make a horizontal crease across the side corners.

⑥ Open and spread.

⑦ Press down folds so that each pleat faces the same direction.

⑧ Make an inner reversed fold at the end of pleat.

⑨ Fold back far corner.

⑩ Repeat on remaining ends.

Colored side

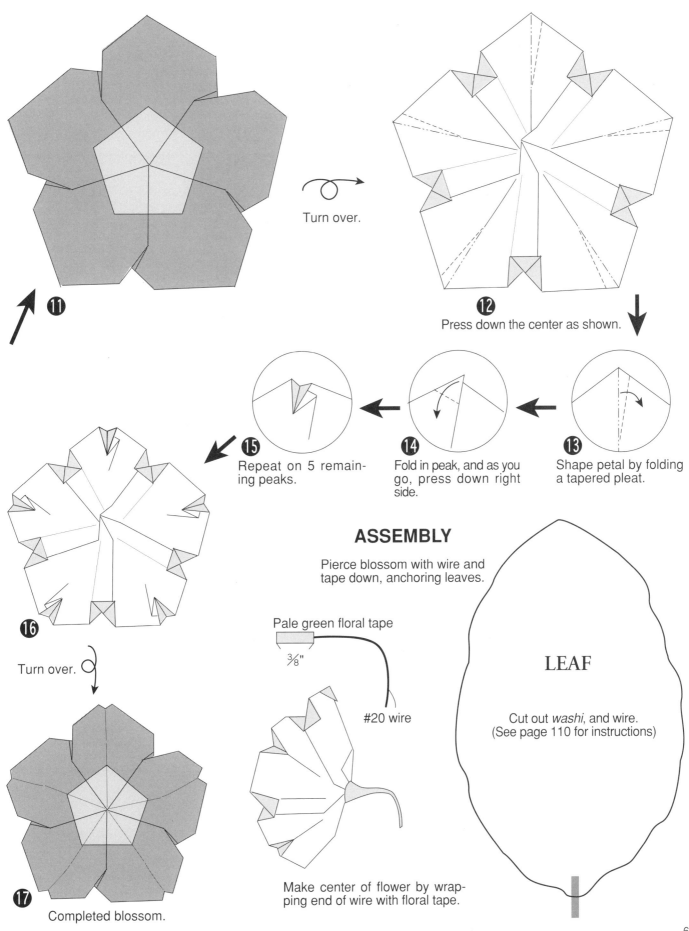

Turn over.

⑪

⑫ Press down the center as shown.

⑮ Repeat on 5 remaining peaks.

⑭ Fold in peak, and as you go, press down right side.

⑬ Shape petal by folding a tapered pleat.

ASSEMBLY

Pierce blossom with wire and tape down, anchoring leaves.

⑯

Turn over.

Pale green floral tape

3/8"

#20 wire

Make center of flower by wrapping end of wire with floral tape.

⑰

Completed blossom.

LEAF

Cut out *washi*, and wire.
(See page 110 for instructions)

GERBERA #1, #2 (Shown on page 14)

Paper materials needed for each blossom
Blossom   : 1 sheet (6", solid or shaded color)
Calyx (cup) : 1 sheet (3", green)
Leaves   : *Washi* paper (green)
Other materials
#24 wrapped floral wire for leaves

⅛" thick wrapped wire (green)
Green floral tape

See page 111 for LEAF PATTERNS.

"Sheet" means a square sheet of origami or similar paper.

GERBERA #1

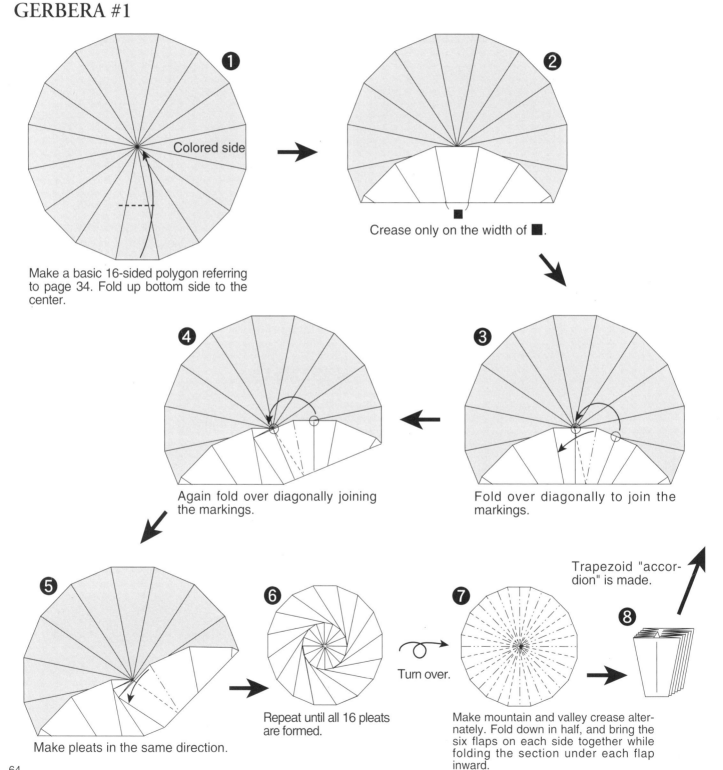

❶ Colored side

Make a basic 16-sided polygon referring to page 34. Fold up bottom side to the center.

❷ Crease only on the width of ■.

❸ Fold over diagonally to join the markings.

❹ Again fold over diagonally joining the markings.

❺ Make pleats in the same direction.

❻ Repeat until all 16 pleats are formed.

Turn over.

❼ Make mountain and valley crease alternately. Fold down in half, and bring the six flaps on each side together while folding the section under each flap inward.

❽ Trapezoid "accordion" is made.

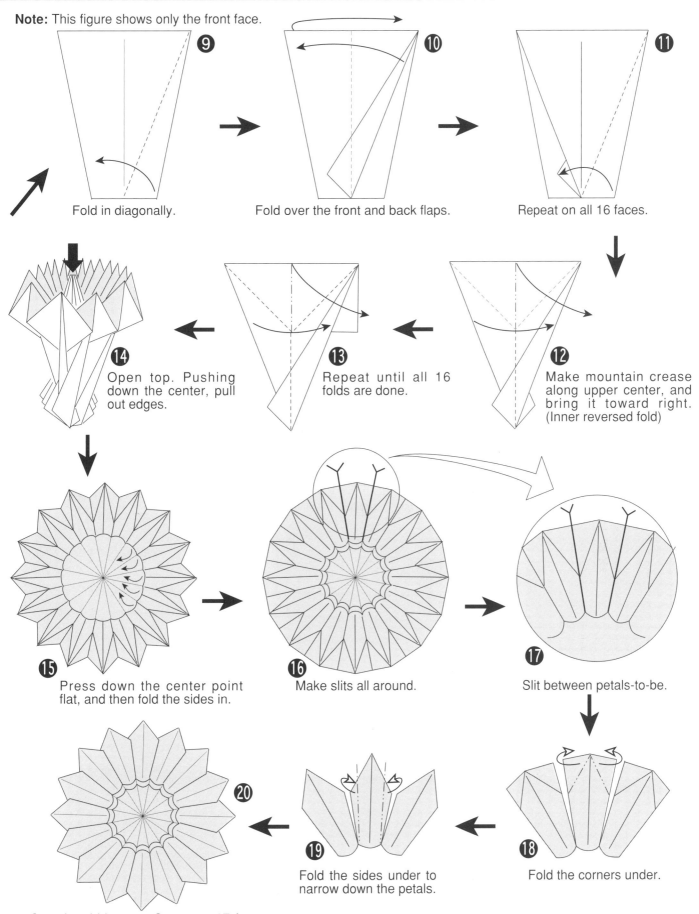

Note: This figure shows only the front face.

9 Fold in diagonally.

10 Fold over the front and back flaps.

11 Repeat on all 16 faces.

12 Make mountain crease along upper center, and bring it toward right. (Inner reversed fold)

13 Repeat until all 16 folds are done.

14 Open top. Pushing down the center, pull out edges.

15 Press down the center point flat, and then fold the sides in.

16 Make slits all around.

17 Slit between petals-to-be.

18 Fold the corners under.

19 Fold the sides under to narrow down the petals.

20 Completed blossom. See page 67 for assembly.

GERBERA #2 (Work as for GERBERA #1 from Step 1 through 11 on previous pages.)

◆**Shown on page 14, Materials on page 64**

⑫

⑬

⑭

⑮ When all petals are folded, shape edges.

Pushing the center, spread out by pulling corners out little by little.

Press down the center point flat, and then fold the sides in.

Using creases made in Steps 10-11, fold tapering pleats in the same direction.

⑯ Make an inner reversed fold on each petal fold.

Repeat all around. Be sure to avoid pointed petals.

⑲

⑱

⑰

Fold lower corner under.

Completed blossom. See opposite page for assembly.

To make a contrasting center:

♥Single center

♥Double center

Unfold the pleats. Color the center using alcohol-based marker, or glue on a round piece of paper of a contrasting color.

Do the same as Single center, and glue on a smaller piece of paper just before folding the rim in.

CALYX(CUP) FOR GERBERA (Use 3" sheet.)

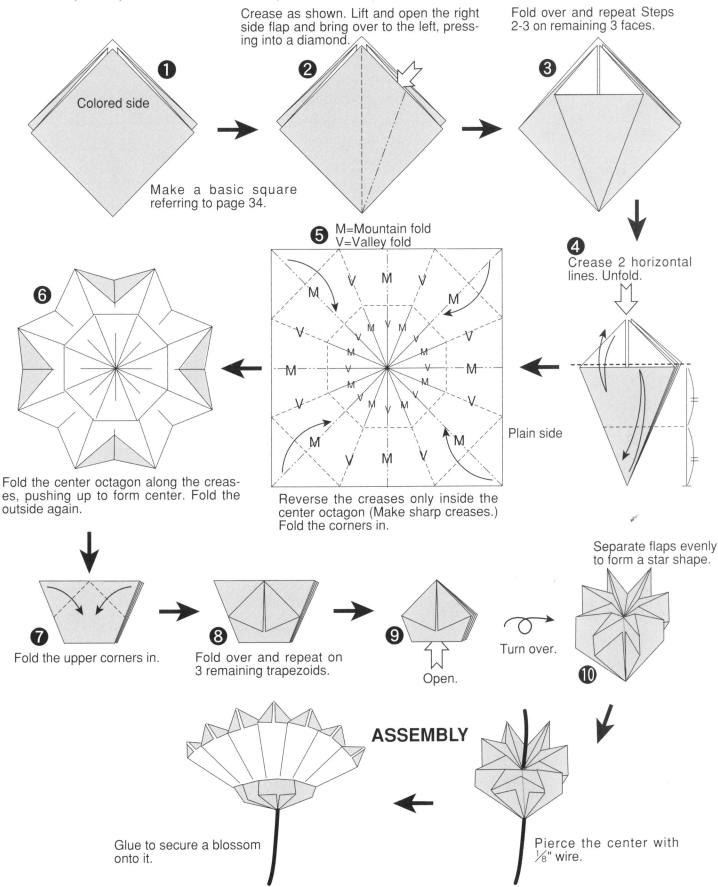

① Colored side

Make a basic square referring to page 34.

② Crease as shown. Lift and open the right side flap and bring over to the left, pressing into a diamond.

③ Fold over and repeat Steps 2-3 on remaining 3 faces.

④ Crease 2 horizontal lines. Unfold.

Plain side

⑤ M=Mountain fold
V=Valley fold

Reverse the creases only inside the center octagon (Make sharp creases.) Fold the corners in.

⑥ Fold the center octagon along the creases, pushing up to form center. Fold the outside again.

⑦ Fold the upper corners in.

⑧ Fold over and repeat on 3 remaining trapezoids.

⑨ Open.

Turn over.

⑩

Separate flaps evenly to form a star shape.

Pierce the center with ⅛" wire.

ASSEMBLY

Glue to secure a blossom onto it.

COSMOS (Shown on page 30)

Paper materials needed for each blossom
Blossom   : 1 sheet (6", solid color)
Calyx(cup) : 1 sheet (3", green *washi* paper)
Leaves   : *Washi* paper (green)
Other materials
Wrapped floral wire: #20 for stems, #24 for leaves

Floral tape (green)
Alcohol-based markers

"Sheet" means a square sheet of origami or similar paper.

BLOSSOM (Work Steps 1 through 8 as for those of Gerbera #1 page 64.)

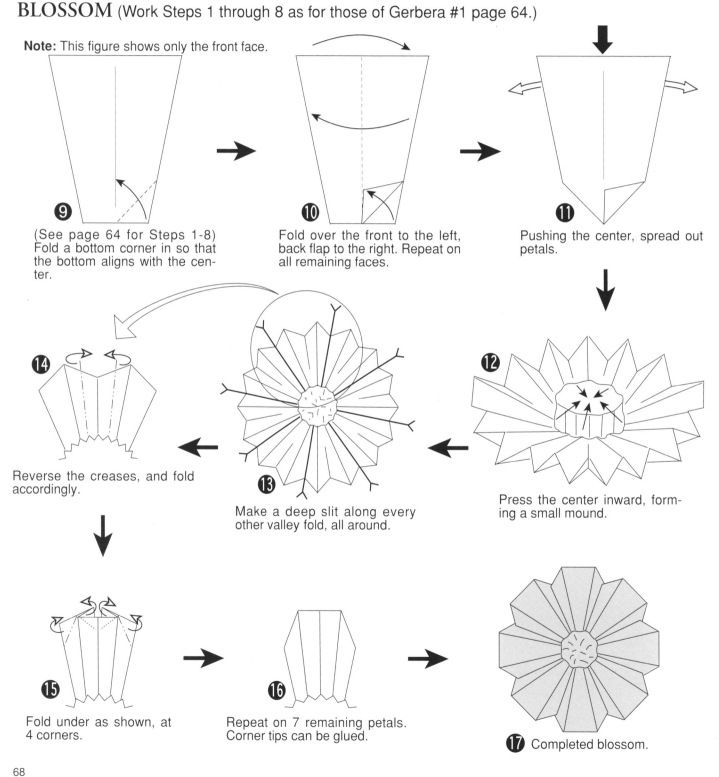

Note: This figure shows only the front face.

⑨ (See page 64 for Steps 1-8) Fold a bottom corner in so that the bottom aligns with the center.

⑩ Fold over the front to the left, back flap to the right. Repeat on all remaining faces.

⑪ Pushing the center, spread out petals.

⑫ Press the center inward, forming a small mound.

⑬ Make a deep slit along every other valley fold, all around.

⑭ Reverse the creases, and fold accordingly.

⑮ Fold under as shown, at 4 corners.

⑯ Repeat on 7 remaining petals. Corner tips can be glued.

⑰ Completed blossom.

CALYX (CUP)

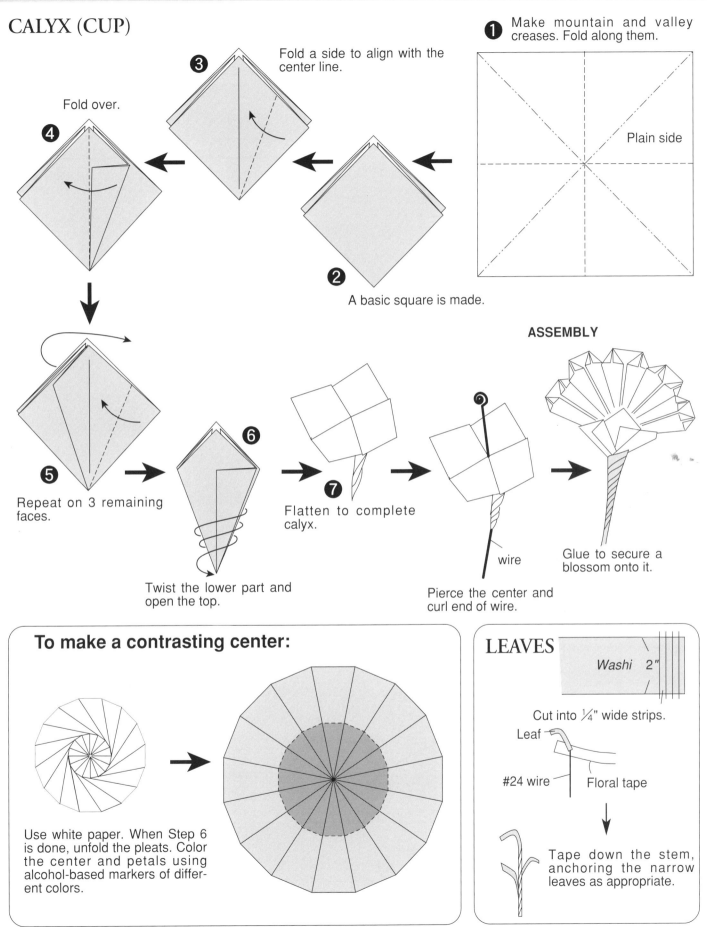

❶ Make mountain and valley creases. Fold along them.

Plain side

❷ A basic square is made.

Fold a side to align with the center line.

❸

Fold over.

❹

❺ Repeat on 3 remaining faces.

Twist the lower part and open the top.

❻

❼ Flatten to complete calyx.

ASSEMBLY

wire

Pierce the center and curl end of wire.

Glue to secure a blossom onto it.

To make a contrasting center:

Use white paper. When Step 6 is done, unfold the pleats. Color the center and petals using alcohol-based markers of different colors.

LEAVES

Washi 2"

Cut into ¼" wide strips.

Leaf

#24 wire   Floral tape

Tape down the stem, anchoring the narrow leaves as appropriate.

GINNIA (Shown on page 15)

Paper materials needed for each blossom
Blossom : 2 sheets (6", solid color)
          : 2 sheets (5" and 4", solid color)
Center : 1 sheet (¾", yellow)
Leaves : *Washi* paper (green)

Other materials
Wrapped floral wire: #18 for stems, #24 for leaves
Floral tape (deep green)

See page 111 for LEAF PATTERNS.

"Sheet" means a square sheet of origami or similar paper.

BLOSSOM (Make a basic 16-sided polygon, and work Steps 1 through 14 of GERBERA #1 on pages 64-65

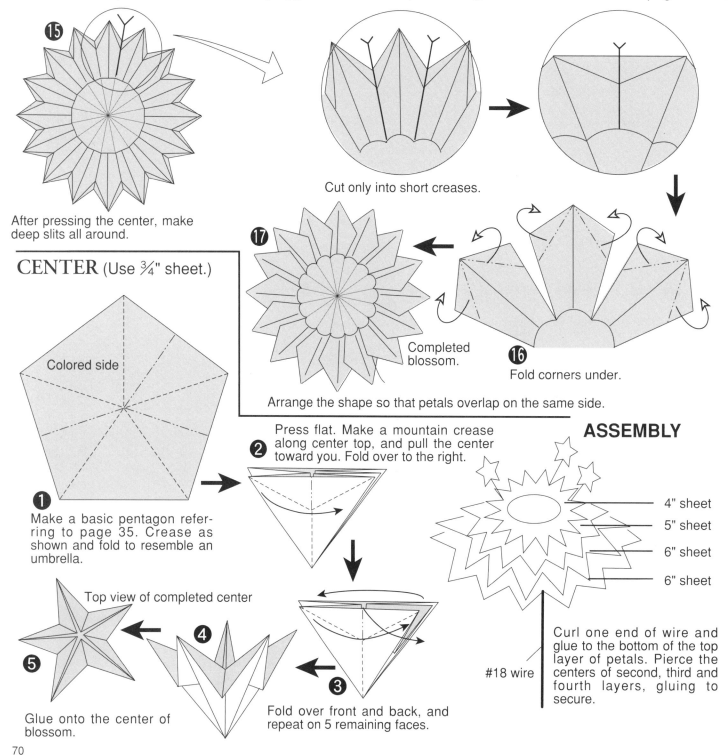

15 After pressing the center, make deep slits all around.

Cut only into short creases.

17 Completed blossom.

Arrange the shape so that petals overlap on the same side.

16 Fold corners under.

CENTER (Use ¾" sheet.)

Colored side

1 Make a basic pentagon referring to page 35. Crease as shown and fold to resemble an umbrella.

2 Press flat. Make a mountain crease along center top, and pull the center toward you. Fold over to the right.

3 Fold over front and back, and repeat on 5 remaining faces.

4 Top view of completed center

5 Glue onto the center of blossom.

ASSEMBLY

4" sheet
5" sheet
6" sheet
6" sheet

#18 wire

Curl one end of wire and glue to the bottom of the top layer of petals. Pierce the centers of second, third and fourth layers, gluing to secure.

SUNFLOWER (Shown on page 22)

Paper materials needed for each blossom, bud and calyx

Blossom : 1 sheet (10" *washi* sheet, yellow)
Center : 1 sheet (4¾" *washi* sheet, dark brown)
Calyx (cup) : 1 sheet (6" *washi* sheet, green)
Bud : 1 sheet (6" *washi* paper, green)
Leaves : *Washi* paper (green)

Other materials

Wrapped floral wire: #20 for stems, #24 for leaves
⅛" thick wrapped wire (green)
Floral tape (deep green)

See page 112 for LEAF PATTERNS.

"Sheet" means a square sheet of origami or similar paper.

CALYX (CUP)

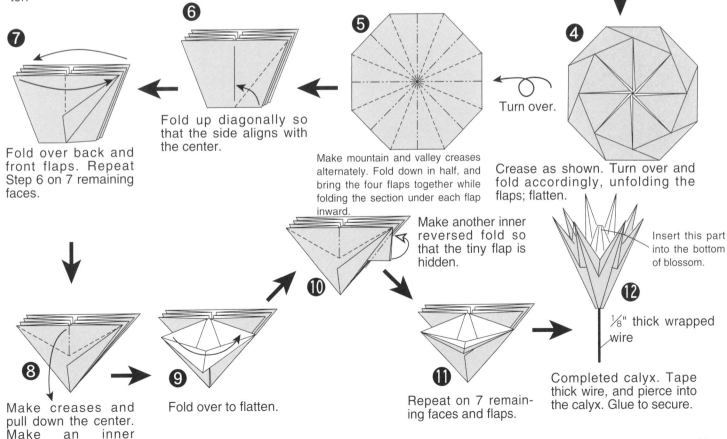

❶

Plain side

Using 6" sheet, make a basic octagon referring to page 35. Fold up so that bottom side meets the center.

❷

Lift and fold so that points ◯ meet up.

❸

Flatten edges. Repeat until all the edges are folded in the same direction. When folding the last edge, lift the first flap and fold over the last, reversing the creases.

❹

Crease as shown. Turn over and fold accordingly, unfolding the flaps; flatten.

Turn over.

❺

Make mountain and valley creases alternately. Fold down in half, and bring the four flaps together while folding the section under each flap inward.

❻

Fold up diagonally so that the side aligns with the center.

❼

Fold over back and front flaps. Repeat Step 6 on 7 remaining faces.

❽

Make creases and pull down the center. Make an inner reversed fold.

❾

Fold over to flatten.

❿

Make another inner reversed fold so that the tiny flap is hidden.

⓫

Repeat on 7 remaining faces and flaps.

⓬

Insert this part into the bottom of blossom.

⅛" thick wrapped wire

Completed calyx. Tape thick wire, and pierce into the calyx. Glue to secure.

BLOSSOM OF SUNFLOWER

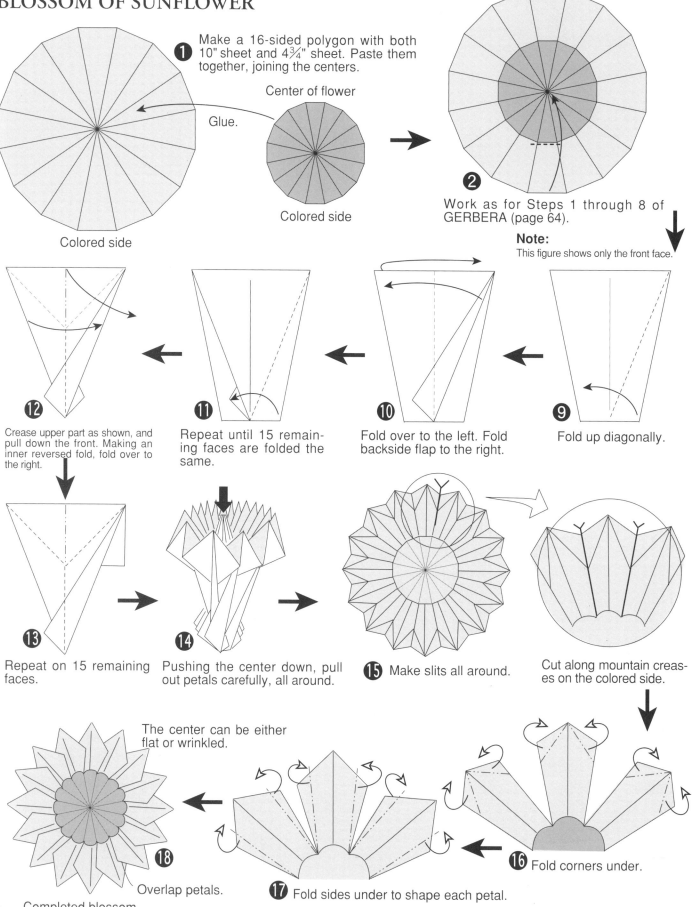

1 Make a 16-sided polygon with both 10" sheet and 4¾" sheet. Paste them together, joining the centers.

Center of flower

Glue.

Colored side

Colored side

Colored side

2 Work as for Steps 1 through 8 of GERBERA (page 64).

Note:
This figure shows only the front face.

12 Crease upper part as shown, and pull down the front. Making an inner reversed fold, fold over to the right.

11 Repeat until 15 remaining faces are folded the same.

10 Fold over to the left. Fold backside flap to the right.

9 Fold up diagonally.

13 Repeat on 15 remaining faces.

14 Pushing the center down, pull out petals carefully, all around.

15 Make slits all around.

Cut along mountain creases on the colored side.

The center can be either flat or wrinkled.

18 Overlap petals. Completed blossom.

17 Fold sides under to shape each petal.

16 Fold corners under.

SUNFLOWER BUD

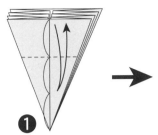

① Using 6" sheet, make an octagon referring to page 35 but just until Step 5. Mark ⅓ from the top, and fold down to crease. Open flat.

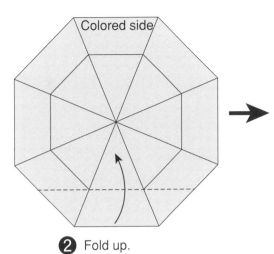

Colored side

② Fold up.

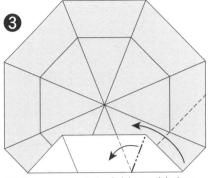

③ Make a mountain fold, and bring it toward you as you fold the next side in.

④ Repeat until all the sides are folded in the same direction.

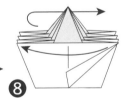

⑤ When folding the last, unfold the first and fold over it.

Turn over.

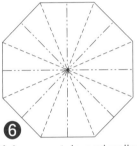

⑥ Make mountain and valley creases as shown. Fold to resemble an umbrella, and press flat.

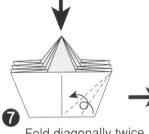

⑦ Fold diagonally twice.

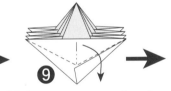

⑧ Fold over front and back. Repeat Steps 7-8 until all faces are done.

⑨ Make creases, and pull the center down to make an inner reversed fold.

⑩ Pull peaks of opposite angles downward, and inflate the center.

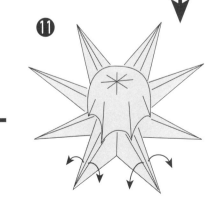

⑪ Unfold and curl the petals.

ASSEMBLY

Insert wrapped wire and glue for completed bud.

⅛" thick wrapped wire

73

MORNING GLORY (Shown on page 20)

Paper materials needed for each blossom, bud and calyx

Blossom : 1 sheet (6", white or solid color)
Bud : 1 sheet (6", white)
Calyx(cup) : 1 sheet (3", green)
Leaves : *Washi* paper (green)

Other materials

Wrapped floral wire: #20 for stems, #24 for leaves
⅛" thick wrapped wire (green)
Floral tape (white and deep green)
Alcohol-based marker

See page 111 for LEAF PATTERNS.

BLOSSOM

"Sheet" means a square sheet of origami or similar paper.

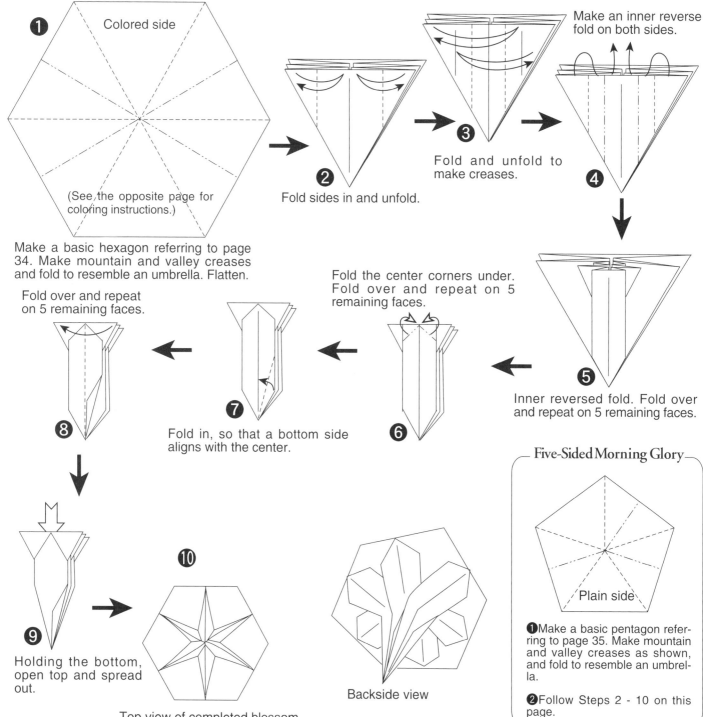

❶ Colored side

(See the opposite page for coloring instructions.)

Make a basic hexagon referring to page 34. Make mountain and valley creases and fold to resemble an umbrella. Flatten.

❷ Fold sides in and unfold.

❸ Fold and unfold to make creases.

Make an inner reverse fold on both sides.

❹

❺ Inner reversed fold. Fold over and repeat on 5 remaining faces.

Fold the center corners under. Fold over and repeat on 5 remaining faces.

❻

❼ Fold in, so that a bottom side aligns with the center.

Fold over and repeat on 5 remaining faces.

❽

❾ Holding the bottom, open top and spread out.

❿ Top view of completed blossom.

Backside view

Five-Sided Morning Glory

Plain side

❶ Make a basic pentagon referring to page 35. Make mountain and valley creases as shown, and fold to resemble an umbrella.

❷ Follow Steps 2 - 10 on this page.

BUD

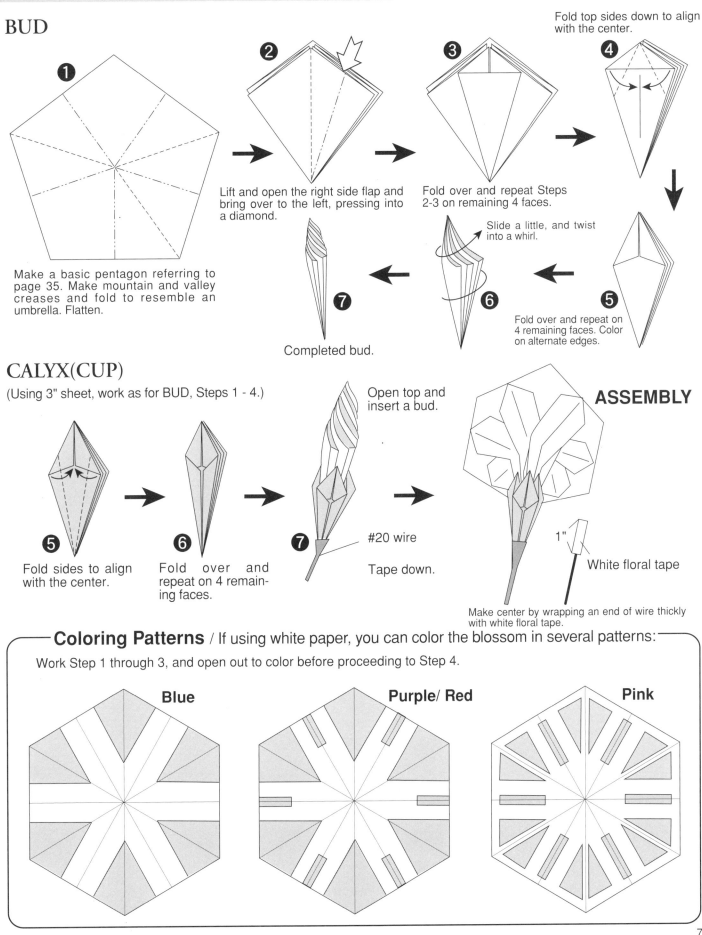

① Make a basic pentagon referring to page 35. Make mountain and valley creases and fold to resemble an umbrella. Flatten.

② Lift and open the right side flap and bring over to the left, pressing into a diamond.

③ Fold over and repeat Steps 2-3 on remaining 4 faces.

④ Fold top sides down to align with the center.

⑤ Fold over and repeat on 4 remaining faces. Color on alternate edges.

⑥ Slide a little, and twist into a whirl.

⑦ Completed bud.

CALYX(CUP)

(Using 3" sheet, work as for BUD, Steps 1 - 4.)

⑤ Fold sides to align with the center.

⑥ Fold over and repeat on 4 remaining faces.

⑦ Open top and insert a bud. #20 wire. Tape down.

ASSEMBLY

1" White floral tape

Make center by wrapping an end of wire thickly with white floral tape.

Coloring Patterns / If using white paper, you can color the blossom in several patterns:

Work Step 1 through 3, and open out to color before proceeding to Step 4.

Blue

Purple/ Red

Pink

DAHLIA (Shown on page 23)

Paper materials needed for each blossom
Large blossom : 4 sheets (6", shaded color)
Small blossom : 4 sheets (3", shaded color)
Leaves : *Washi* paper (green)
Other materials
Wrapped floral wire: #18 for stems, #24 for leaves

Floral tape (green)
See page 112 for LEAF PATTERNS.

"Sheet" means a square sheet of origami or similar paper.

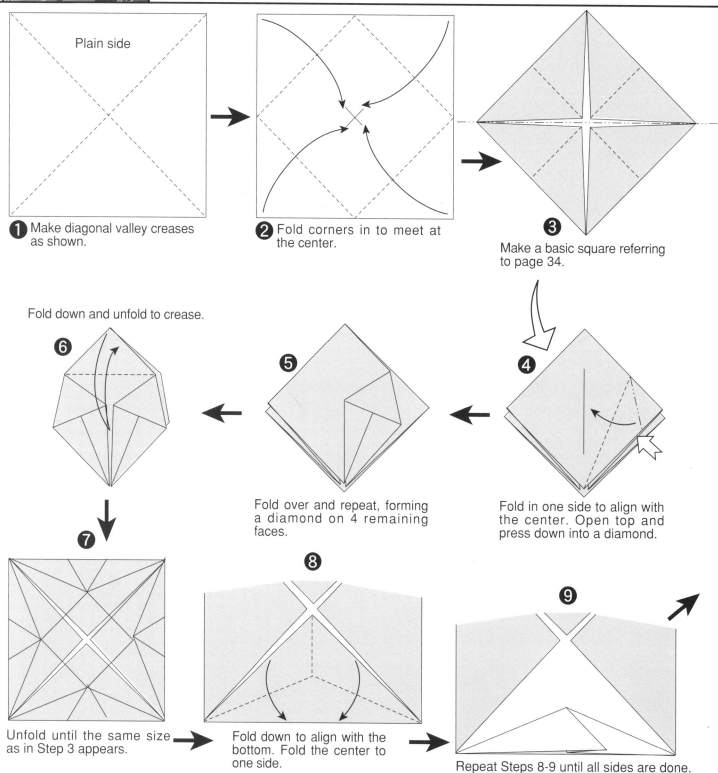

Plain side

❶ Make diagonal valley creases as shown.

❷ Fold corners in to meet at the center.

❸ Make a basic square referring to page 34.

❹ Fold in one side to align with the center. Open top and press down into a diamond.

❺ Fold over and repeat, forming a diamond on 4 remaining faces.

Fold down and unfold to crease.

❻

❼ Unfold until the same size as in Step 3 appears.

❽ Fold down to align with the bottom. Fold the center to one side.

❾ Repeat Steps 8-9 until all sides are done.

BUD OF JAPANESE IRIS (Use 6" sheet.)

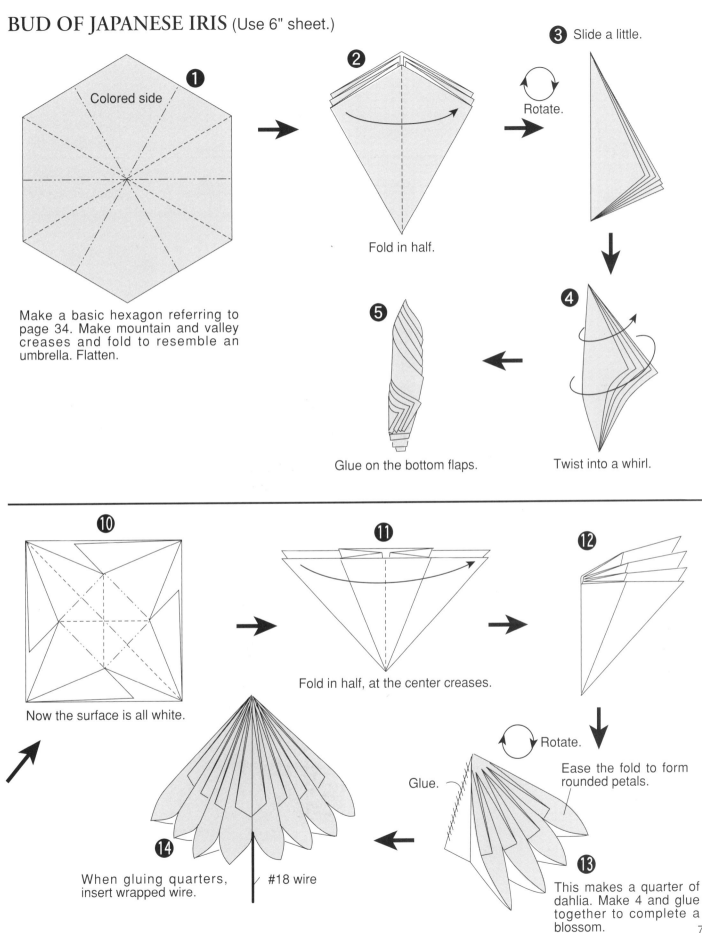

① Colored side

Make a basic hexagon referring to page 34. Make mountain and valley creases and fold to resemble an umbrella. Flatten.

② Fold in half.

③ Slide a little.

Rotate.

④ Twist into a whirl.

⑤ Glue on the bottom flaps.

⑩ Now the surface is all white.

⑪ Fold in half, at the center creases.

⑫

Rotate.

Ease the fold to form rounded petals.

⑬ This makes a quarter of dahlia. Make 4 and glue together to complete a blossom.

Glue.

⑭ When gluing quarters, insert wrapped wire.

#18 wire

JAPANESE IRIS (Shown on page 16)

Paper materials needed for each blossom, bud and calyx

Blossom : 2 sheets (6", white)
Bud : 1 sheet (4", white)
Calyx (cup) : 1 sheet (6", white)
Leaves : *Washi* paper (green)

Other materials

Wrapped floral wire: #20 for leaves
1/8" thick wrapped wire (green)
Floral tape (green)
Alcohol-based markers

See page 112 for LEAF PATTERNS.

BLOSSOM

"Sheet" means a square sheet of origami or similar paper.

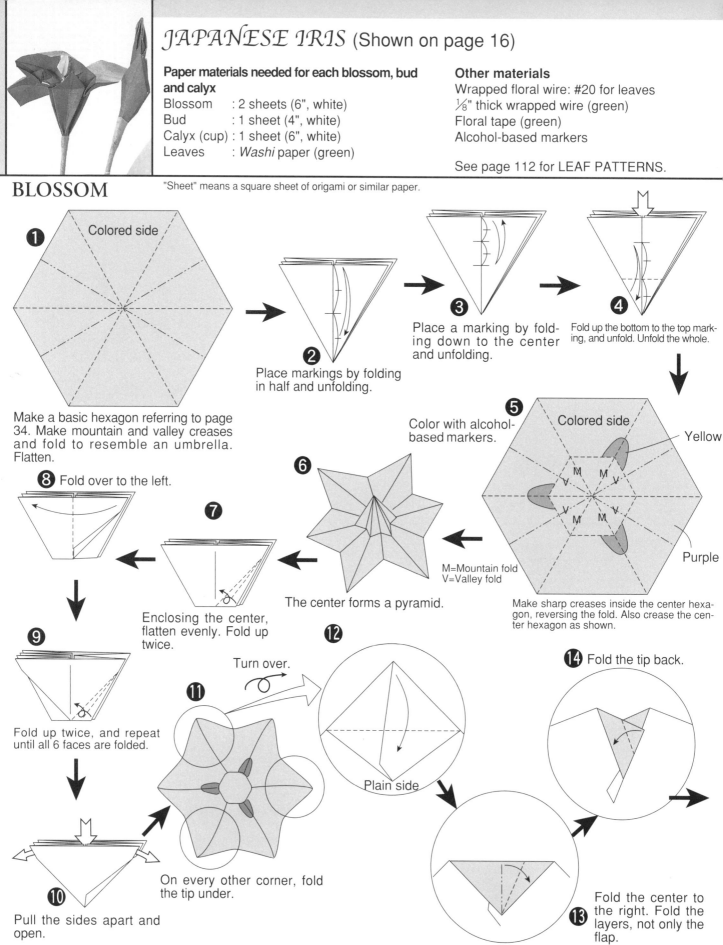

① Colored side

Make a basic hexagon referring to page 34. Make mountain and valley creases and fold to resemble an umbrella. Flatten.

② Place markings by folding in half and unfolding.

③ Place a marking by folding down to the center and unfolding.

④ Fold up the bottom to the top marking, and unfold. Unfold the whole.

⑤ Colored side · Yellow · Purple · Color with alcohol-based markers.

M=Mountain fold
V=Valley fold

Make sharp creases inside the center hexagon, reversing the fold. Also crease the center hexagon as shown.

⑥ The center forms a pyramid.

⑦ Enclosing the center, flatten evenly. Fold up twice.

⑧ Fold over to the left.

⑨ Fold up twice, and repeat until all 6 faces are folded.

⑩ Pull the sides apart and open.

⑪ On every other corner, fold the tip under.

⑫ Turn over. · Plain side

⑬ Fold the center to the right. Fold the layers, not only the flap.

⑭ Fold the tip back.

78

CALYX (CUP) FOR BUD

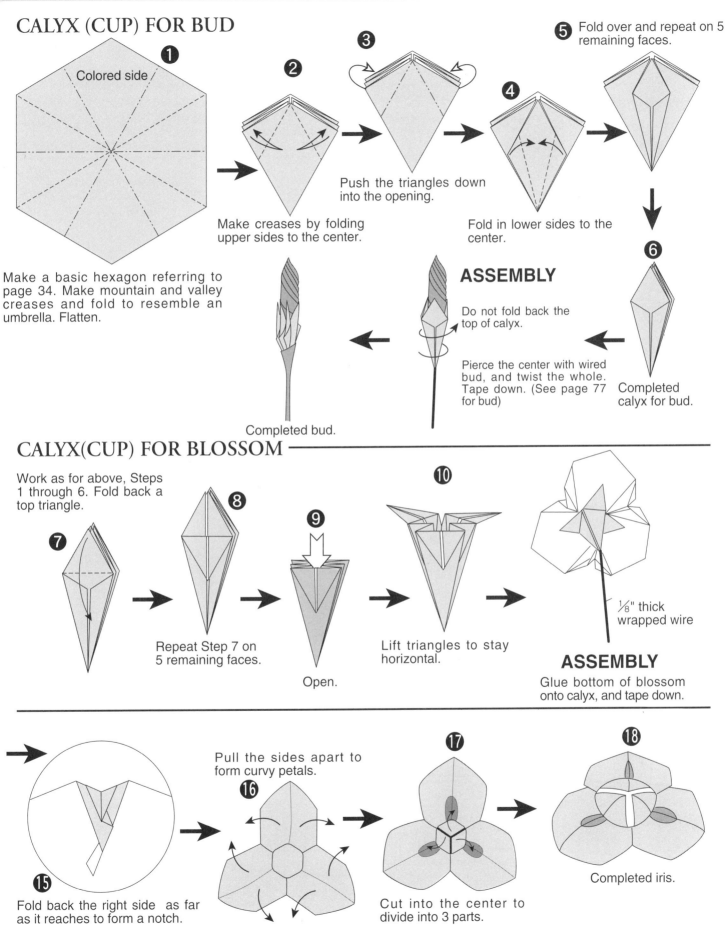

1 Colored side

Make a basic hexagon referring to page 34. Make mountain and valley creases and fold to resemble an umbrella. Flatten.

2 Make creases by folding upper sides to the center.

3 Push the triangles down into the opening.

4 Fold in lower sides to the center.

5 Fold over and repeat on 5 remaining faces.

6 Completed calyx for bud.

ASSEMBLY

Do not fold back the top of calyx.

Pierce the center with wired bud, and twist the whole. Tape down. (See page 77 for bud)

Completed bud.

CALYX(CUP) FOR BLOSSOM

Work as for above, Steps 1 through 6. Fold back a top triangle.

7

8 Repeat Step 7 on 5 remaining faces.

9 Open.

10 Lift triangles to stay horizontal.

ASSEMBLY

Glue bottom of blossom onto calyx, and tape down.

⅛" thick wrapped wire

15 Fold back the right side as far as it reaches to form a notch.

16 Pull the sides apart to form curvy petals.

17 Cut into the center to divide into 3 parts.

18 Completed iris.

HOLLYHOCK (Shown on page 17)

Paper materials needed for each blossom, bud and calyx

Blossom   : 2 sheets (6", solid color)
Center   : 1 sheet (2", light green)
Pistil   : 1 sheet (3", yellow)
Bud   : 1 sheet (3", light green)
Calyx (cup) : 1 sheet (3", light green)

Leaves   : *Washi* paper (green)
Other materials
Wrapped floral wire: #20 for stems, #24 for leaves
1/8" thick wrapped wire (green)
Floral tape (green)

"Sheet" means a square sheet of origami or similar paper.

BLOSSOM

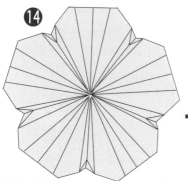

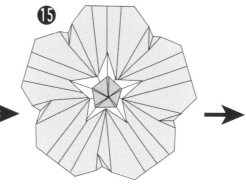

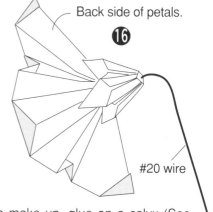

Back side of petals.

#20 wire

14 Make 2 basic pentagons and paste them together, plain sides facing in. Work as for STOCK (p50-51), Steps 1 through 13.

15 Make a center and pistil (see below), and glue them onto the blossom.

16 To make up, glue on a calyx (See opposite page), and pierce with wire. Glue to secure.

CENTER

Make a basic pentagon referring to page 35. Fold corners in.

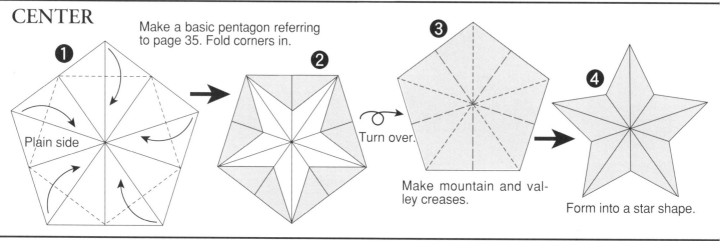

1 Plain side

2

Turn over.

3 Make mountain and valley creases.

4 Form into a star shape.

PISTIL

Make a basic pentagon referring to page 35 Make mountain and valley creases. Fold accordingly to resemble an umbrella. Flatten.

Fold in so that upper side aligns with the center.

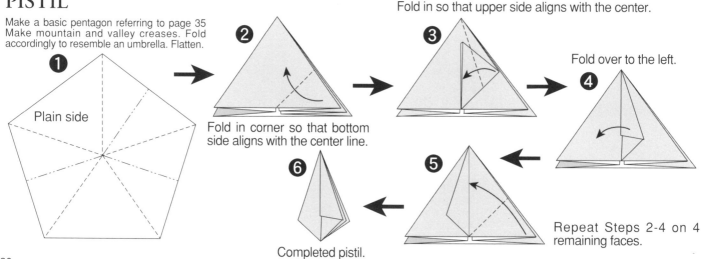

1 Plain side

2 Fold in corner so that bottom side aligns with the center line.

3

4 Fold over to the left.

5

6 Completed pistil.

Repeat Steps 2-4 on 4 remaining faces.

80

BUD / CALYX

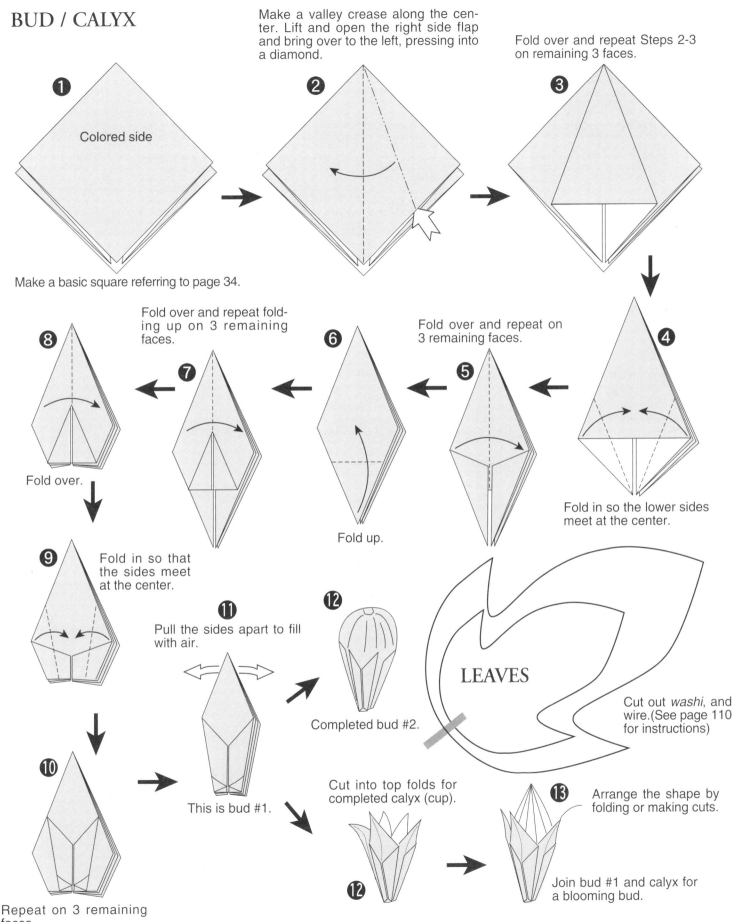

① Colored side

Make a basic square referring to page 34.

② Make a valley crease along the center. Lift and open the right side flap and bring over to the left, pressing into a diamond.

③ Fold over and repeat Steps 2-3 on remaining 3 faces.

④ Fold in so the lower sides meet at the center.

⑤ Fold over and repeat on 3 remaining faces.

⑥ Fold up.

⑦ Fold over and repeat folding up on 3 remaining faces.

⑧ Fold over.

⑨ Fold in so that the sides meet at the center.

⑩ Repeat on 3 remaining faces.

⑪ Pull the sides apart to fill with air.

This is bud #1.

⑫ Completed bud #2.

Cut into top folds for completed calyx (cup).

⑫

LEAVES

Cut out *washi*, and wire.(See page 110 for instructions)

⑬ Arrange the shape by folding or making cuts.

Join bud #1 and calyx for a blooming bud.

HYDRANGEA (Shown on page 18)

Paper materials needed for each cluster
Floret : 9 sheets (2¼", solid color)
        : 6-7 sheets (3", solid color)
Leaves : *Washi* paper (green)
Other materials
#24 wrapped floral wire for stems and leaves

⅛" thick wrapped wire (green)
Floral tape (green)

See opposite page for LEAF PATTERNS.

"Sheet" means a square sheet of origami or similar paper.

STERILE FLORET(Large petals)

Make a basic square referring to page 34. Fold up the bottom and unfold to make a crease. Open.

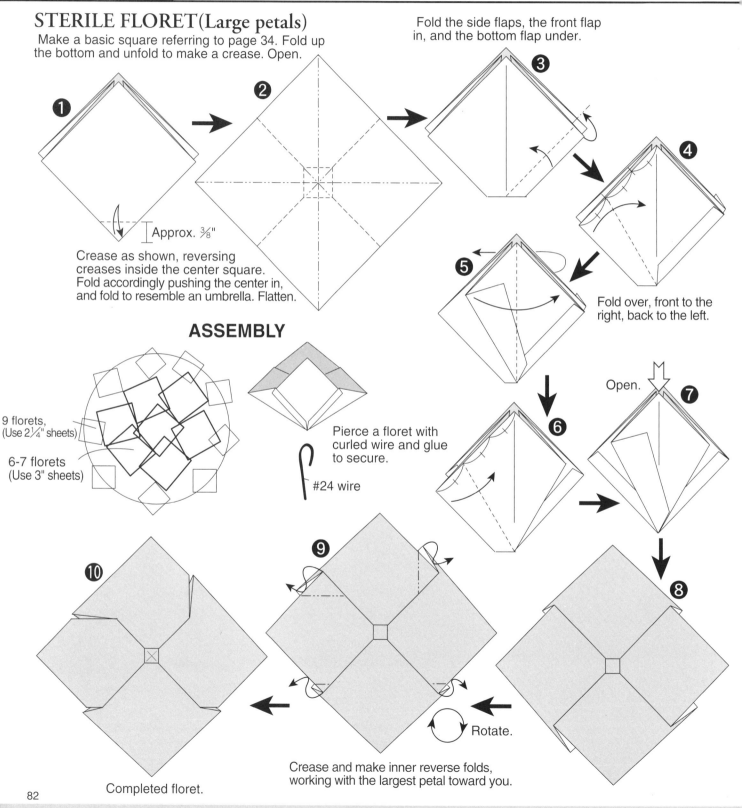

❶ Approx. ⅜"

Crease as shown, reversing creases inside the center square. Fold accordingly pushing the center in, and fold to resemble an umbrella. Flatten.

❷

Fold the side flaps, the front flap in, and the bottom flap under.

❸

❹

❺ Fold over, front to the right, back to the left.

❻

❼ Open.

ASSEMBLY

9 florets,
(Use 2¼" sheets)

6-7 florets
(Use 3" sheets)

Pierce a floret with curled wire and glue to secure.

#24 wire

❽

❾

Rotate.

❿ Completed floret.

Crease and make inner reverse folds, working with the largest petal toward you.

82

LACE CAP HYDRANGEA (Shown on page 18)

Paper materials needed for each cluster
Sterile florets : 9-14 sheets (3", pastel color)
Fertile florets : 9-14 sheets (3", both pastel color and light green)
Leaves : *Washi* paper (green)
Other materials
#24 wrapped floral wire for stems and leaves

⅛" thick wrapped wire (green)
Floral tape (deep green)

"Sheet" means a square sheet of origami or similar paper.

FERTILE FLORET (Small, starry petals)

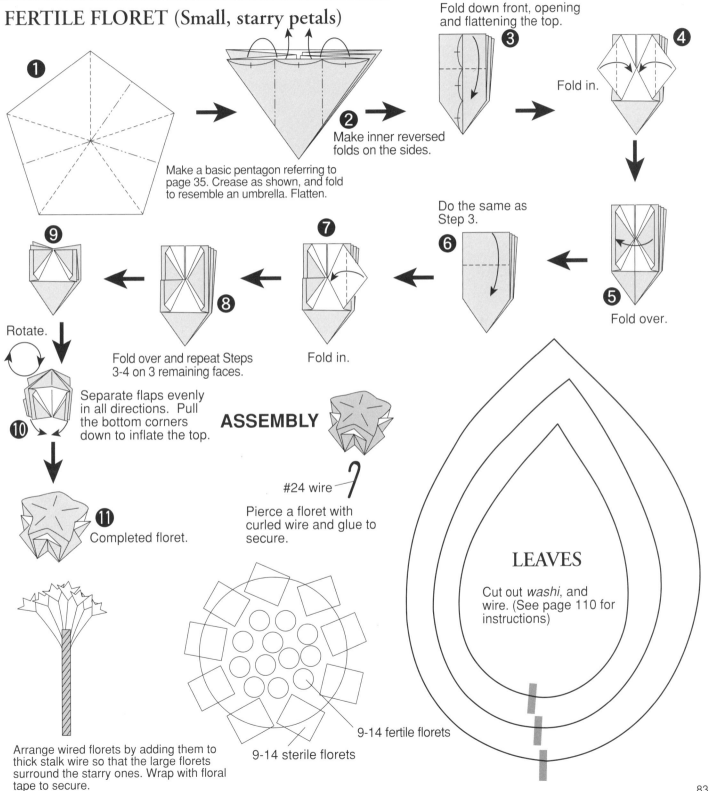

❶ Make a basic pentagon referring to page 35. Crease as shown, and fold to resemble an umbrella. Flatten.

❷ Make inner reversed folds on the sides.

❸ Fold down front, opening and flattening the top.

❹ Fold in.

❺ Fold over.

❻ Do the same as Step 3.

❼ Fold in.

❽ Fold over and repeat Steps 3-4 on 3 remaining faces.

❾ Rotate.

❿ Separate flaps evenly in all directions. Pull the bottom corners down to inflate the top.

⓫ Completed floret.

ASSEMBLY

#24 wire
Pierce a floret with curled wire and glue to secure.

Arrange wired florets by adding them to thick stalk wire so that the large florets surround the starry ones. Wrap with floral tape to secure.

9-14 fertile florets

9-14 sterile florets

LEAVES

Cut out *washi*, and wire. (See page 110 for instructions)

BLUE STAR (Shown on page 19)

Paper materials needed for each blossom and bud

Blossom : 1 sheet (3", pastel color)
Bud   : 1 sheet (1½", pale green or pastel)
Leaves : *Washi* paper (green)

Other materials

#24 wrapped floral wire for stems and leaves
⅛" thick wrapped wire (green)
Floral tape (green)

"Sheet" means a square sheet of origami or similar paper.

BLOSSOM

1 Colored side

Make a basic pentagon referring to page 35. Make mountain and valley creases and fold to resemble an umbrella. Flatten.

2 Fold in half and unfold to crease. Unfold the whole.

3 Colored side

Fold up using the creases, bringing the bottom to the center.

4 Make a mountain fold, and bring it toward you as you fold the next side in.

5

Repeat with the next side. Continue until all 5 sides are folded.

6 When folding the last corner, lift the first flap and fold over the last, reversing the creases.

Fold in diagonally.

7 Make mountain and valley creases. Turn over and fold accordingly to resemble an umbrella, pulling the flaps.

Turn over.

8

9 Fold over, and repeat folding in on 4 remaining faces.

10 Pull the center and crease.

CALYX (CUP)

❶

Make a basic pentagon. Fold a corner to the center.

❷

Fold the next corner in the same manner. Repeat until all the corners are folded in the same direction. When folding the last corner, lift the first flap and fold over the last, reversing the creases.

❸

Make mountain and valley folds alternately, and fold to resemble an umbrella.

❹

Completed calyx.

ASSEMBLY

Pierce bud with wire and glue. Pierce calyx and glue. Tape down.

#24 wire

Cut out *washi,* and wire.(See page 10 for instructions)

Thrust curled wire into the bottom of bud or blossom, and glue. Thread and tape down.

#24 wire

LEAVES

BUD

Work as for stock bud (page 52), using 2" sheet for pastel bud, and 1½" sheet for green bud. Wire green bud without adding calyx.

⓫

As you pull it down, fold over making a wide "V" shape crease. Repeat on 4 remaining faces. Do not make sharp creases on these petals.

⓬

Catch the center fold and fold to one side. Repeat on all remaining folds.

⓭ Completed blue star.

BEGONIA (Shown on page 21)

Paper materials needed for each floret
Blossom : 1 sheet (2", solid or shaded color)
Center : 1 sheet (½", yellow)
Floral leaf : 1 sheet (½", shaded color)
Leaves : *Washi* paper (green)

"Sheet" means a square sheet of origami or similar paper.

Other materials
#24 wrapped floral wire for stems and leaves
⅛" thick wrapped wire (green)
Floral tape (deep green)

See page 111 for LEAF PATTERNS.

BLOSSOM

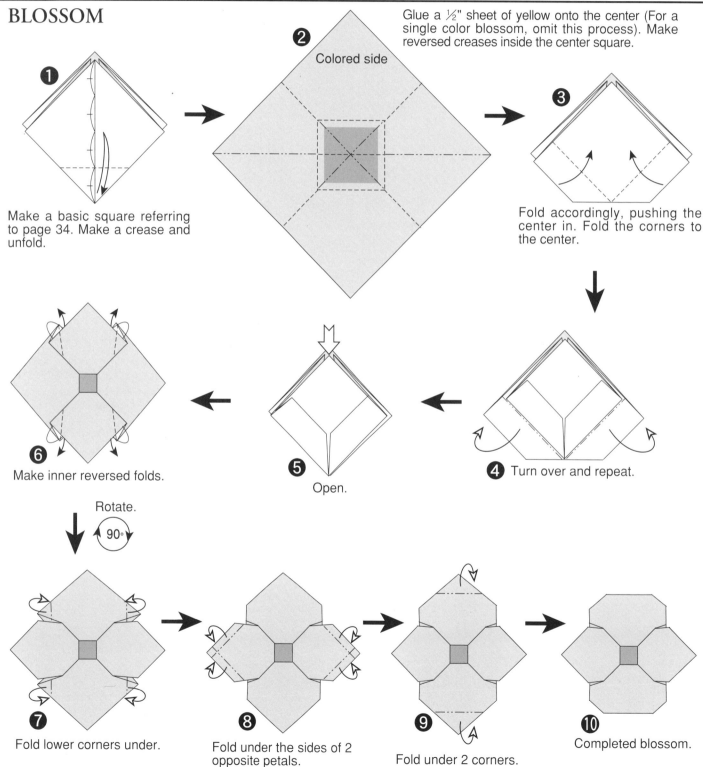

Glue a ½" sheet of yellow onto the center (For a single color blossom, omit this process). Make reversed creases inside the center square.

❶ Make a basic square referring to page 34. Make a crease and unfold.

❷ Colored side

❸ Fold accordingly, pushing the center in. Fold the corners to the center.

❹ Turn over and repeat.

❺ Open.

❻ Make inner reversed folds.

Rotate.
90°

❼ Fold lower corners under.

❽ Fold under the sides of 2 opposite petals.

❾ Fold under 2 corners.

❿ Completed blossom.

FLORAL LEAF #1

❶ Fold corners to the center.

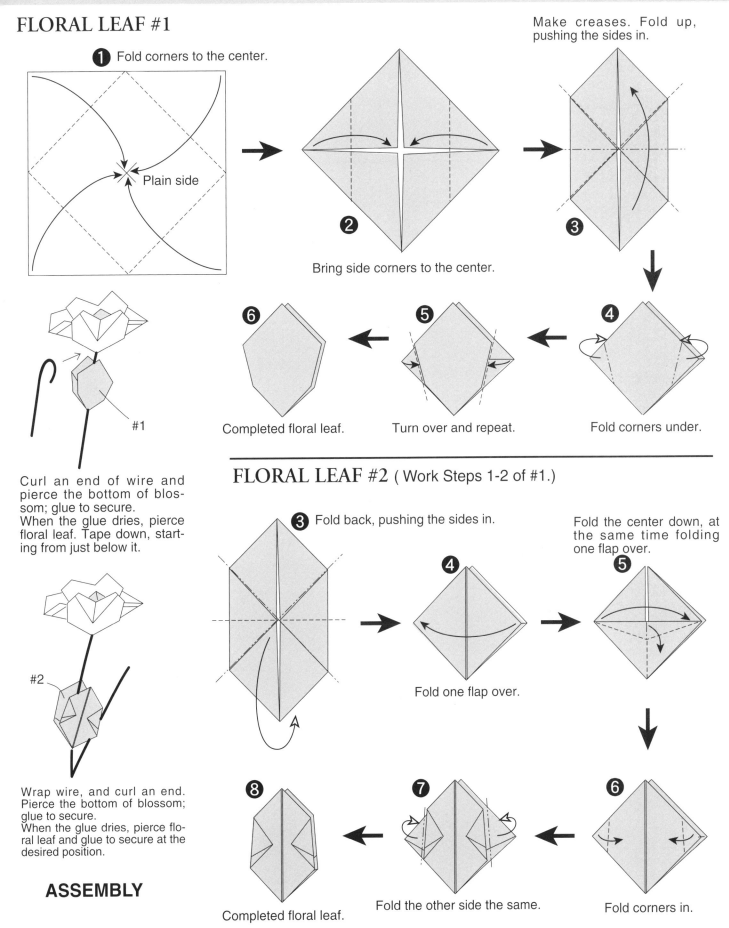

Make creases. Fold up, pushing the sides in.

Plain side

❷

Bring side corners to the center.

❸

❹

Fold corners under.

❺

Turn over and repeat.

❻

Completed floral leaf.

#1

Curl an end of wire and pierce the bottom of blossom; glue to secure.
When the glue dries, pierce floral leaf. Tape down, starting from just below it.

FLORAL LEAF #2 (Work Steps 1-2 of #1.)

❸ Fold back, pushing the sides in.

Fold the center down, at the same time folding one flap over.

❹

Fold one flap over.

❺

❻

Fold corners in.

❼

Fold the other side the same.

❽

Completed floral leaf.

#2

Wrap wire, and curl an end. Pierce the bottom of blossom; glue to secure.
When the glue dries, pierce floral leaf and glue to secure at the desired position.

ASSEMBLY

CINBIDIUM ORCHID (Shown on page 27)

Paper materials needed for each floret
#1: 1 sheet (3", pearly white)
    1 sheet (1½", shaded color)
#2: 1 sheet (4", yellow)
    1 sheet (2", silid color)
#3: 1 sheet (5", wine)
    1 sheet (2½", shaded color)
Leaves : *Washi* paper (green)

Other materials
#20 wrapped floral wire for stems
⅛" thick wrapped wire (green)
Floral tape (green)

See page 112 for LEAF PATTERNS.

"Sheet" means a square sheet of origami or similar paper.

CINBIDIUM ORCHID #1

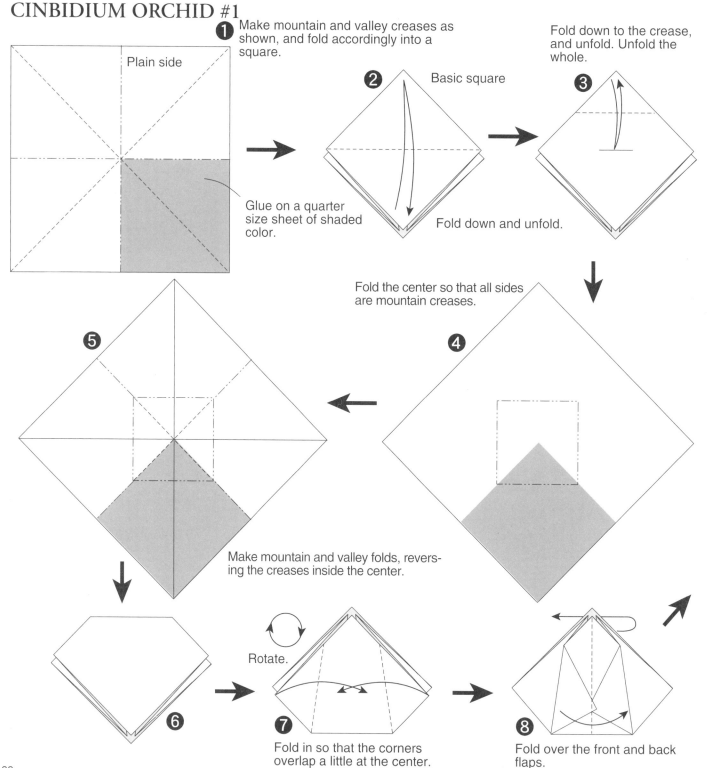

❶ Make mountain and valley creases as shown, and fold accordingly into a square.

Plain side

Glue on a quarter size sheet of shaded color.

❷ Basic square

Fold down and unfold.

❸ Fold down to the crease, and unfold. Unfold the whole.

❹ Fold the center so that all sides are mountain creases.

❺ Make mountain and valley folds, reversing the creases inside the center.

❻

❼ Rotate.

Fold in so that the corners overlap a little at the center.

❽ Fold over the front and back flaps.

Fold back front and back corners.

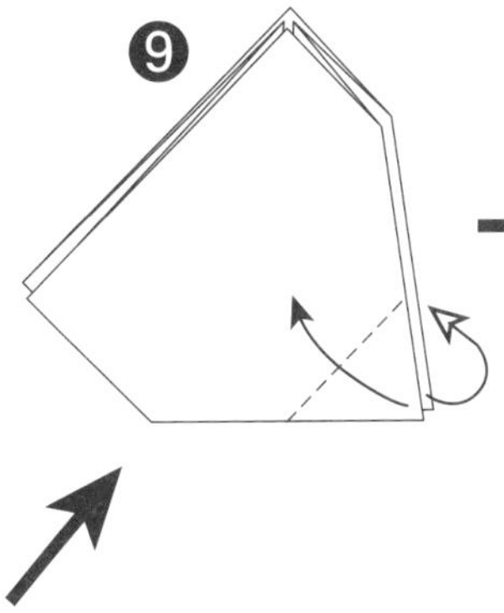

9

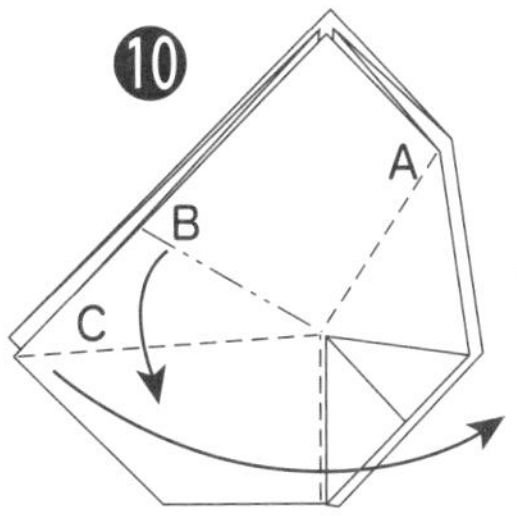

10

Crease A, B and C. While pulling the crease B toward you, fold C across to the right.

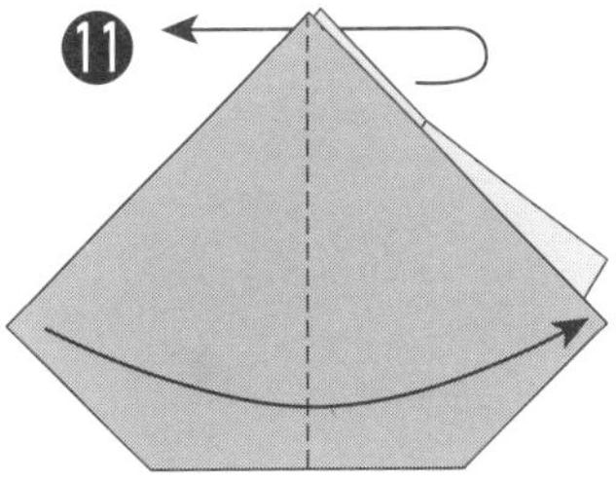

11

Fold over front and back.

Do the same as Step 10, this time reversing direction.

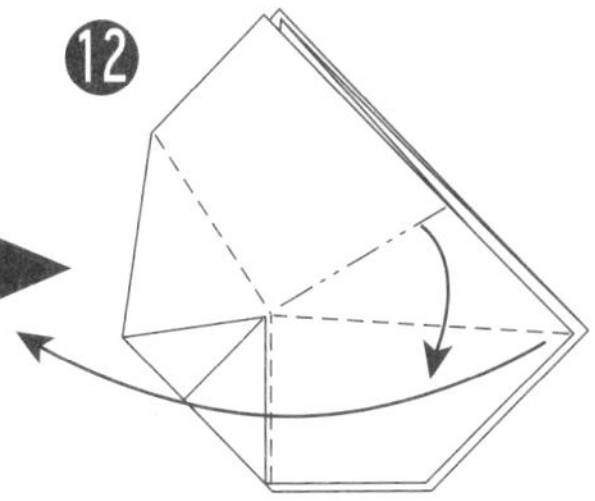

12

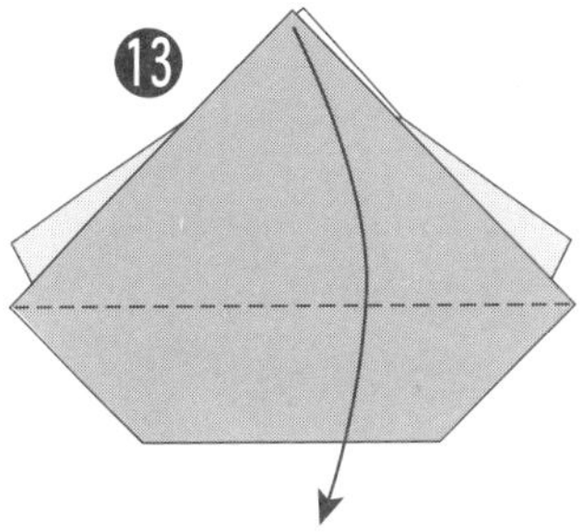

13

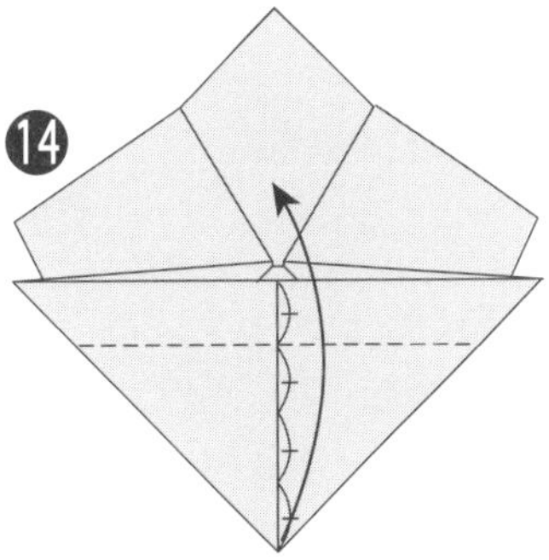

14

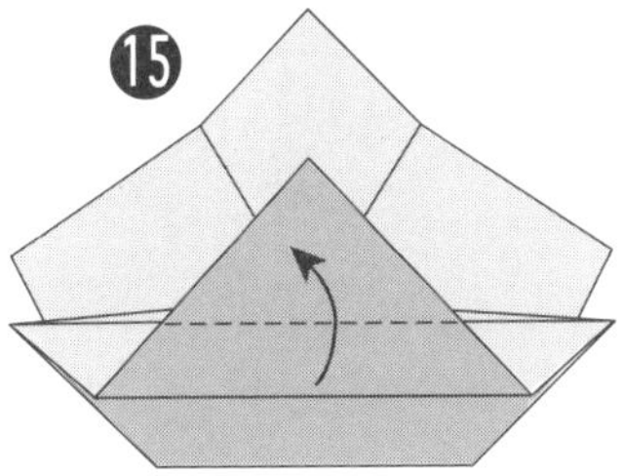

15

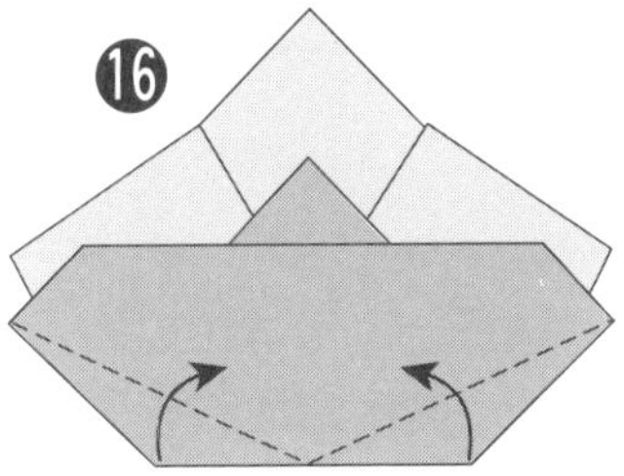

16

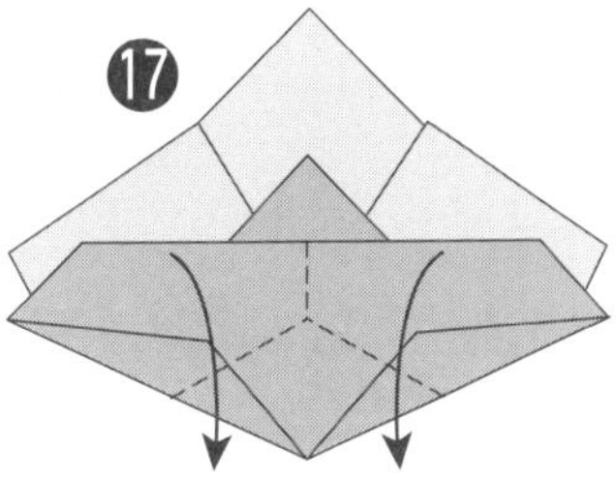

17

Fold the side sections inward so as to protrude toward you. This makes "lip" petal.

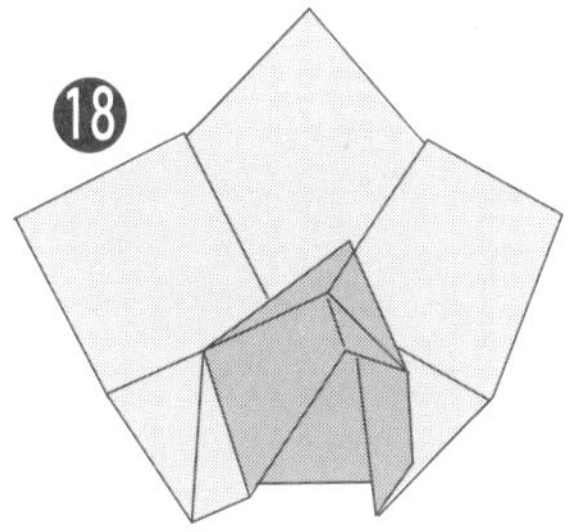

18

Completed floret.

ASSEMBLY

Curl an end of wire and pierce the center of floret; glue to secure.

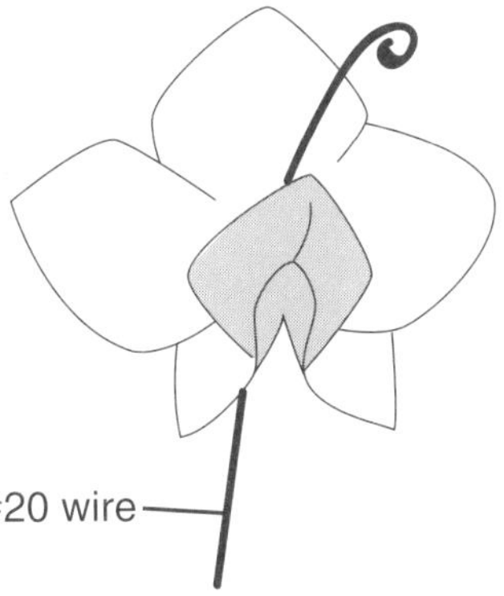

Approx. 4" of #20 wire

Attach stemmed florets to thick wrapped wire with floral tape, checking the balance. Avoid overlapping the florets.

⅛" thick, Wrapped floral wire

CINBIDIUM ORCHID #2 (For Steps 1 - 6, see page 88.)

◆**Shown on page 27, Materials on page 88**

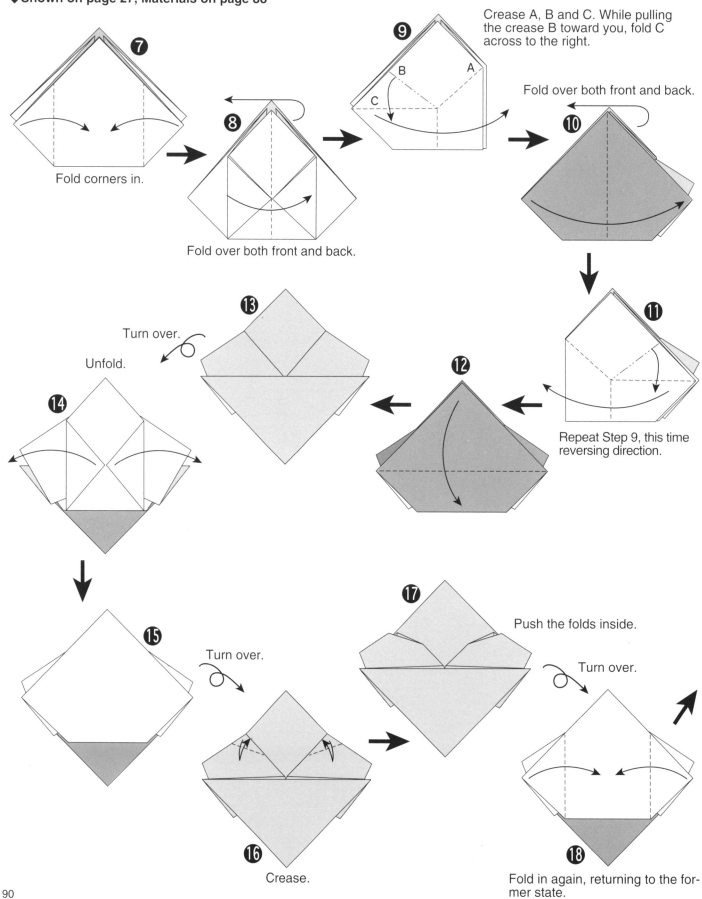

7 Fold corners in.

8 Fold over both front and back.

9 Crease A, B and C. While pulling the crease B toward you, fold C across to the right.

10 Fold over both front and back.

11 Repeat Step 9, this time reversing direction.

12

13

Turn over.

Unfold.

14

15 Turn over.

16 Crease.

17 Push the folds inside.

Turn over.

18 Fold in again, returning to the former state.

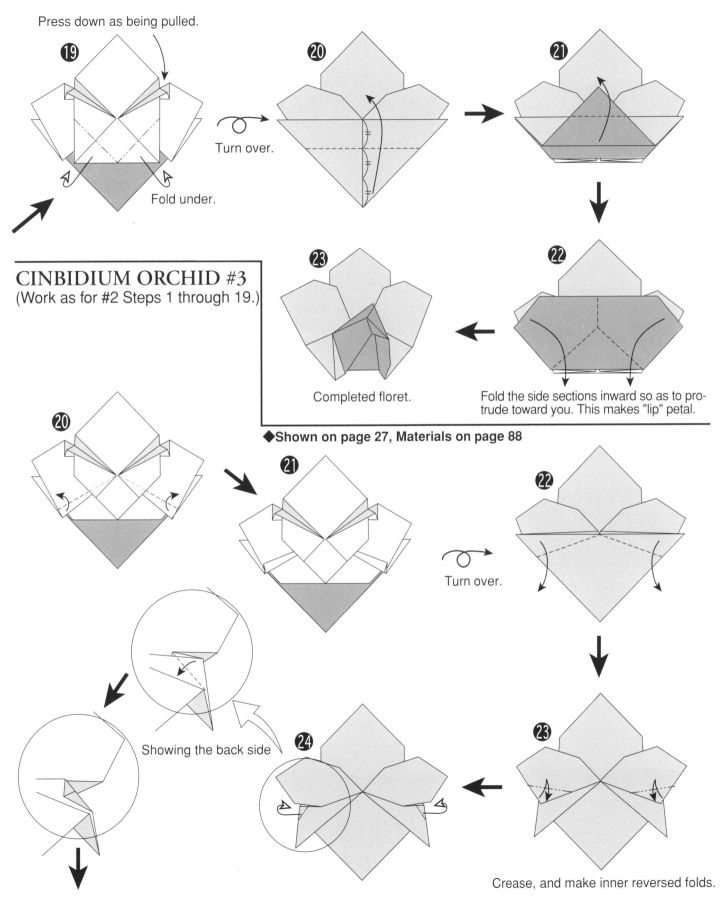

Press down as being pulled.

⑲ Fold under.

Turn over. ⑳

㉑

㉒ Fold the side sections inward so as to protrude toward you. This makes "lip" petal.

㉓ Completed floret.

CINBIDIUM ORCHID #3
(Work as for #2 Steps 1 through 19.)

◆Shown on page 27, Materials on page 88

⑳

㉑

Turn over. ㉒

Showing the back side

㉓

㉔ Crease, and make inner reversed folds.

Continued to page 92 (bottom).

OPENING BLOSSOM OF SPRAY MUM

(Paste a 2" sheet of green onto the center. With the colored side down, work as for BLOSSOM on the opposite page, following Steps 1 through 7.)

  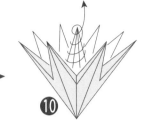 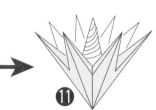

8 Crease and pull the center toward you.

9 Fold the creases as you fold over sideways. Repeat on 7 faces.

10 Twist the center.

11 Completed blooming blossom.

FOUR STATES OF FLOWERS

Insert bottom of each into a calyx (cup) and glue to secure. (See page 94 for calyx.)

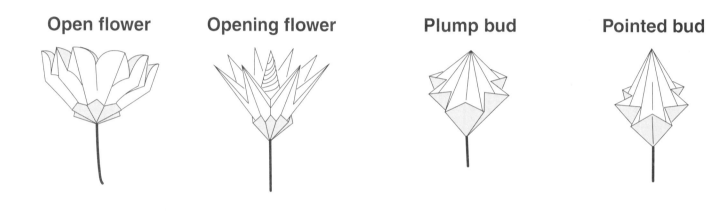

Open flower **Opening flower** **Plump bud** **Pointed bud**

CINBIDIUM ORCHID #3 (Continued from previous page)

Fold the side sections inward so as to protrude toward you. This makes "lip" petal.

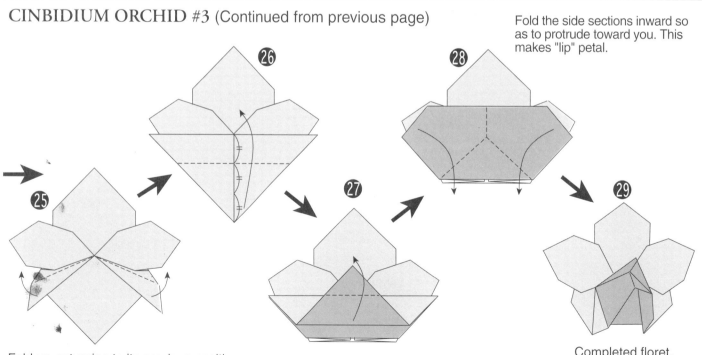

25 Fold up, returning to its previous position.

26

27

28

29 Completed floret.

SPRAY MUM (Shown on page 28)

Paper materials needed for each blossom, bud and calyx
Blossom : 1 sheet (6", solid color)
Center : 1 sheet (2", green)
Plump bud : 1 sheet (3", pale color)
Pointed bud : 1 sheet (2", orange)
Calyx (cup) : 1 (3", green)
Leaves : *Washi* paper (green)

Other materials
Wrapped floral wire: #18 for stems, #20 for leaves
Floral tape (deep green)

See page 111 for LEAF PATTERNS.

"Sheet" means a square sheet of origami or similar paper.

BLOSSOM (Paste 2" sheet onto the center. Make a basic octagon referring to page 35.)

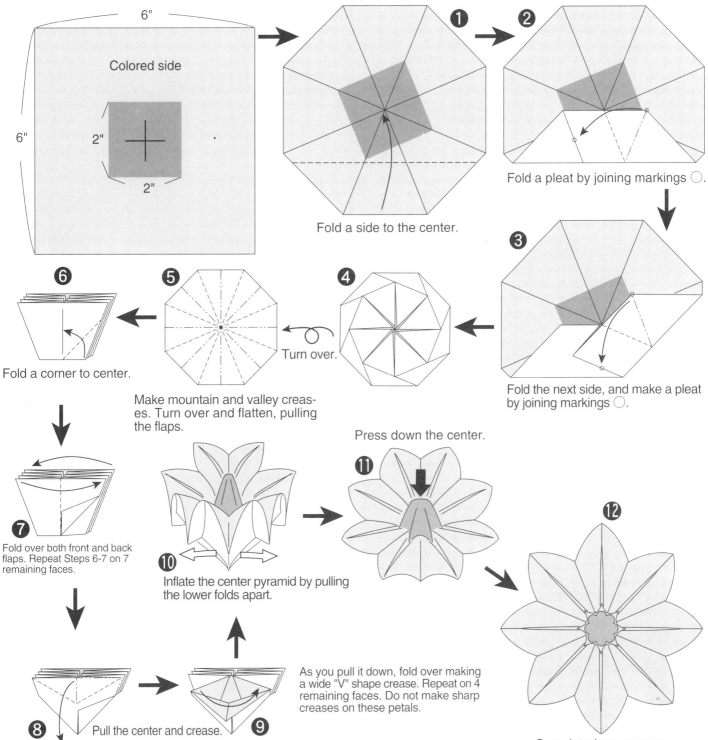

6"

Colored side

6"

2"

2"

① Fold a side to the center.

② Fold a pleat by joining markings ○.

③ Fold the next side, and make a pleat by joining markings ○.

④

Turn over.

⑤ Make mountain and valley creases. Turn over and flatten, pulling the flaps.

⑥ Fold a corner to center.

⑦ Fold over both front and back flaps. Repeat Steps 6-7 on 7 remaining faces.

⑧ Pull the center and crease. **⑨**

⑩ Inflate the center pyramid by pulling the lower folds apart.

As you pull it down, fold over making a wide "V" shape crease. Repeat on 4 remaining faces. Do not make sharp creases on these petals.

Press down the center.

⑪

⑫ Completed spray mum.

PLUMP BUD FOR SPRAY MUM
(Using 3" sheet, colored side down, work as for BLOSSOM on the previous page, following Steps 1 through 5.)

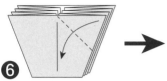

6 Fold diagonally so that a top side aligns with the center line.

7 Fold up diagonally so that the bottom side aligns with the center.

8 Fold over, and repeat on 7 remaining faces.

9 Separate folds evenly for completed bud.

POINTED BUD FOR SPRAY MUM
(Using 2" sheet, colored side down, work Steps 1 through 4 of basic octagon on page 35.)

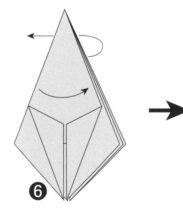

5 Fold in so that bottom sides meet at the center.

6 Fold over 2 flaps on front and back, and fold the same on 3 remaining faces.

7 Separate folds evenly for completed bud.

CALYX (CUP) FOR SPRAY MUM
(Colored side down, work as for BLOSSOM on the previous page, following Steps 1 through 5.)

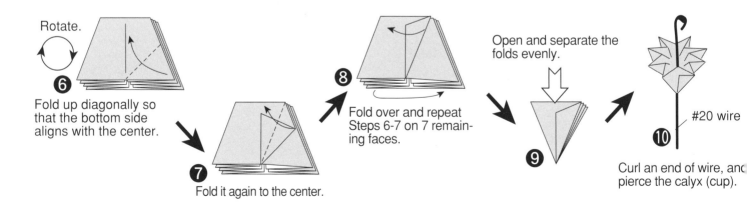

Rotate.

6 Fold up diagonally so that the bottom side aligns with the center.

7 Fold it again to the center.

8 Fold over and repeat Steps 6-7 on 7 remaining faces.

Open and separate the folds evenly.

9

10 #20 wire

Curl an end of wire, and pierce the calyx (cup).

COLORING PATTERNS FOR CLEMATIS BLOSSOMS

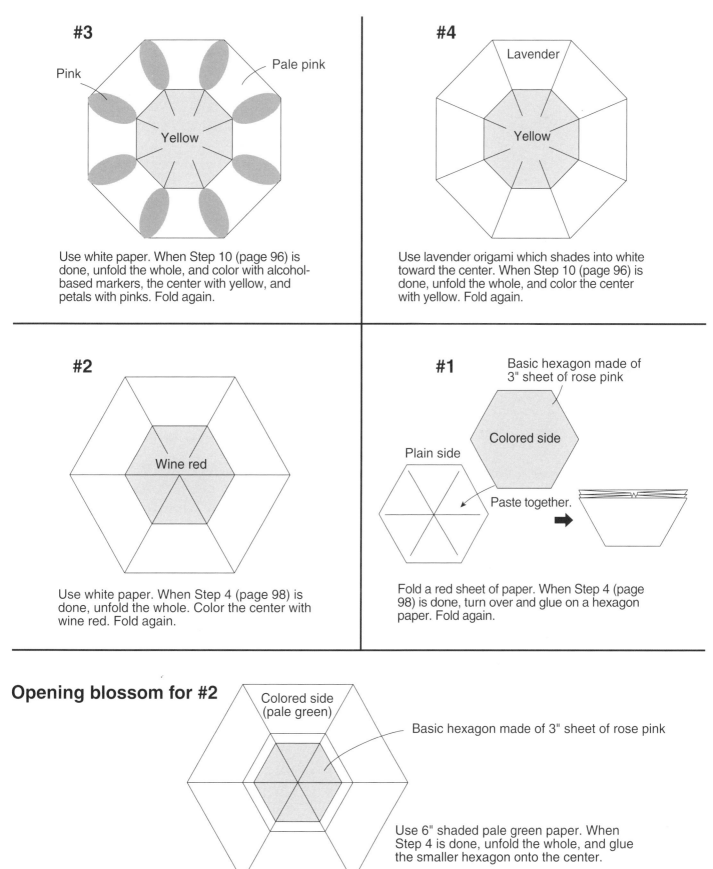

#3

Pink

Pale pink

Yellow

Use white paper. When Step 10 (page 96) is done, unfold the whole, and color with alcohol-based markers, the center with yellow, and petals with pinks. Fold again.

#4

Lavender

Yellow

Use lavender origami which shades into white toward the center. When Step 10 (page 96) is done, unfold the whole, and color the center with yellow. Fold again.

#2

Wine red

Use white paper. When Step 4 (page 98) is done, unfold the whole. Color the center with wine red. Fold again.

#1

Basic hexagon made of 3" sheet of rose pink

Colored side

Plain side

Paste together.

Fold a red sheet of paper. When Step 4 (page 98) is done, turn over and glue on a hexagon paper. Fold again.

Opening blossom for #2

Colored side (pale green)

Basic hexagon made of 3" sheet of rose pink

Use 6" shaded pale green paper. When Step 4 is done, unfold the whole, and glue the smaller hexagon onto the center.

CLEMATIS (Shown on page 26-27)

Paper materials needed for each blossom and bud
Blossom : 1 sheet (6", solid or shaded color)
Center : 1 sheet (3", shaded color))
Bud #1 : 1 sheet (3", solid color)
Bud #2 : 1 sheet (2¼", shaded color)
Leaves : *Washi* paper (deep green)

Other materials
Wrapped floral wire: #20 for stems, #24 for leaves
Floral tape (deep green)
Alcohol-based markers

See page 111 for leaf patterns.

BLOSSOM #3 (Eight narrow petals)

"Sheet" means a square sheet of origami or similar paper.

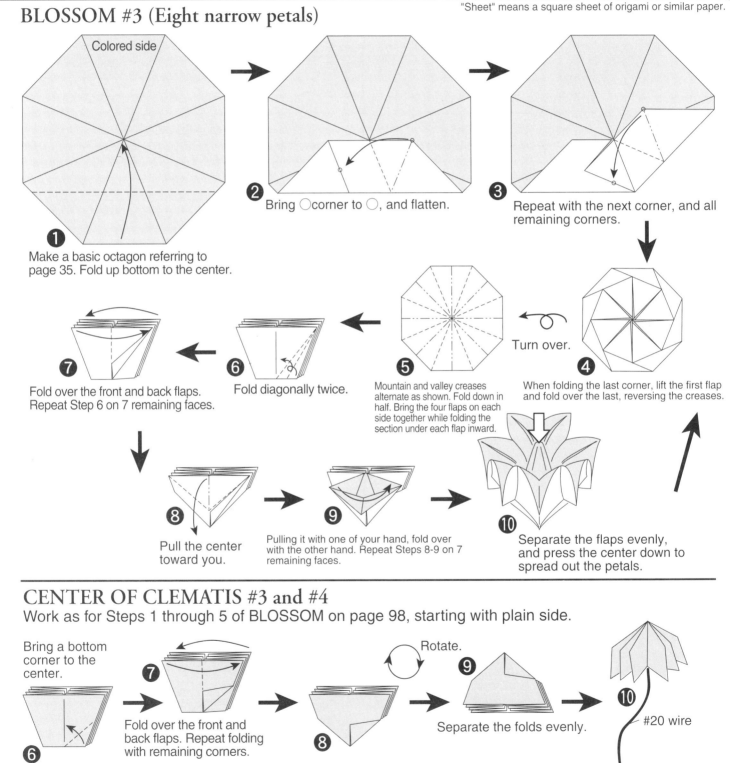

① Make a basic octagon referring to page 35. Fold up bottom to the center.

Colored side

② Bring ◯corner to ◯, and flatten.

③ Repeat with the next corner, and all remaining corners.

④ When folding the last corner, lift the first flap and fold over the last, reversing the creases.

Turn over.

⑤ Mountain and valley creases alternate as shown. Fold down in half. Bring the four flaps on each side together while folding the section under each flap inward.

⑥ Fold diagonally twice.

⑦ Fold over the front and back flaps. Repeat Step 6 on 7 remaining faces.

⑧ Pull the center toward you.

⑨ Pulling it with one of your hand, fold over with the other hand. Repeat Steps 8-9 on 7 remaining faces.

⑩ Separate the flaps evenly, and press the center down to spread out the petals.

CENTER OF CLEMATIS #3 and #4

Work as for Steps 1 through 5 of BLOSSOM on page 98, starting with plain side.

⑥ Bring a bottom corner to the center.

⑦ Fold over the front and back flaps. Repeat folding with remaining corners.

⑧

⑨ Separate the folds evenly.

Rotate.

⑩ #20 wire

Completed center of clematis #3 and #4

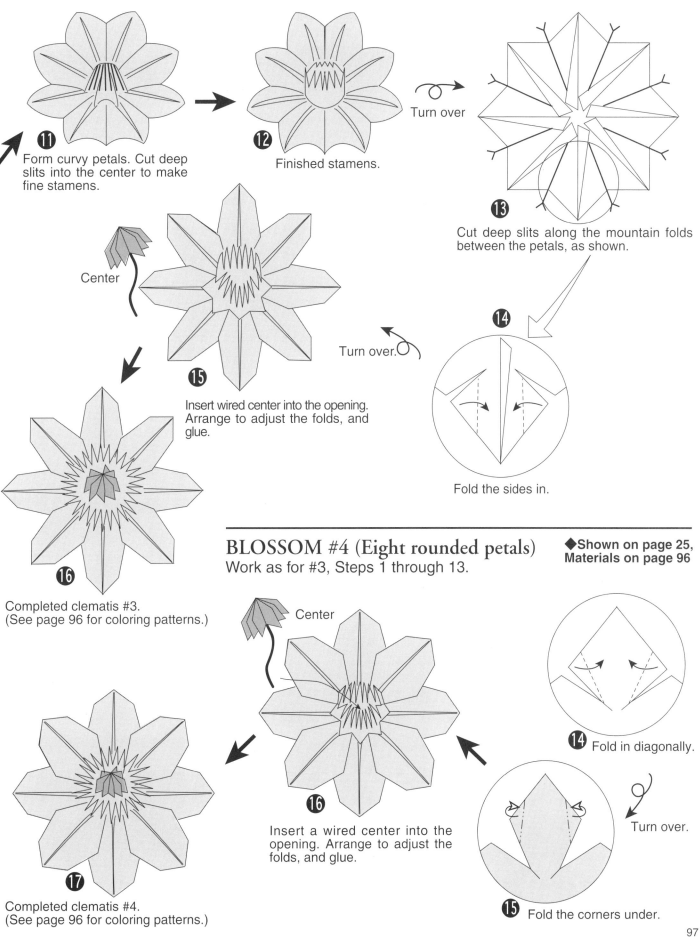

⑪ Form curvy petals. Cut deep slits into the center to make fine stamens.

⑫ Finished stamens.

Turn over

⑬ Cut deep slits along the mountain folds between the petals, as shown.

Center

⑮ Insert wired center into the opening. Arrange to adjust the folds, and glue.

Turn over.

⑭ Fold the sides in.

⑯ Completed clematis #3. (See page 96 for coloring patterns.)

BLOSSOM #4 (Eight rounded petals)
Work as for #3, Steps 1 through 13.

◆ Shown on page 25, Materials on page 96

Center

⑯ Insert a wired center into the opening. Arrange to adjust the folds, and glue.

⑭ Fold in diagonally.

Turn over.

⑮ Fold the corners under.

⑰ Completed clematis #4. (See page 96 for coloring patterns.)

BLOSSOM #1 (Six petals)

◆**Shown on page 24, Materials on page 96**

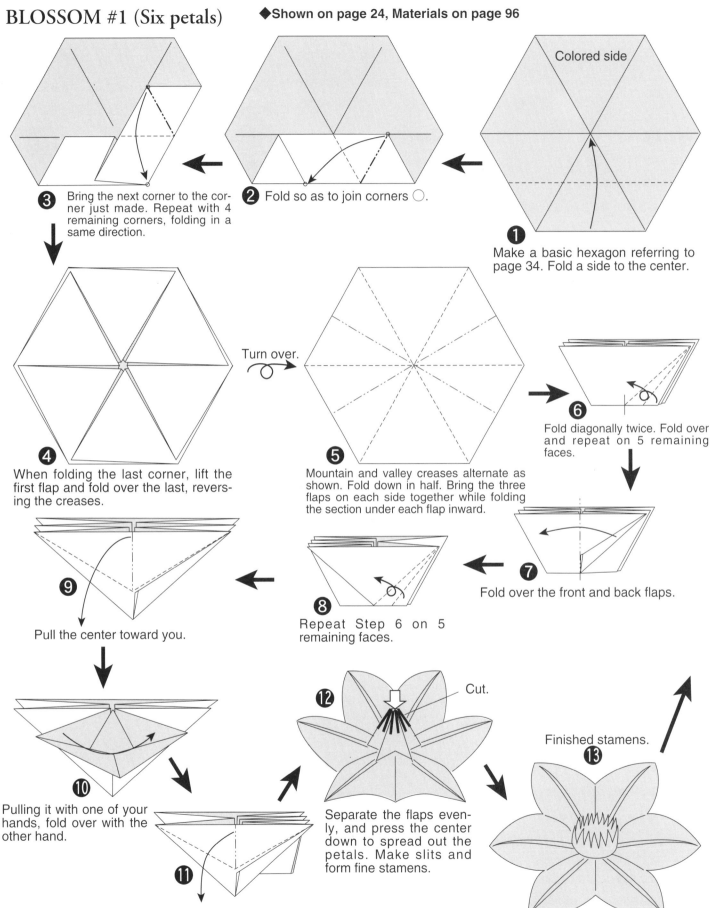

❸ Bring the next corner to the corner just made. Repeat with 4 remaining corners, folding in a same direction.

❷ Fold so as to join corners ○.

❶ Make a basic hexagon referring to page 34. Fold a side to the center.

Colored side

❹ When folding the last corner, lift the first flap and fold over the last, reversing the creases.

Turn over.

❺ Mountain and valley creases alternate as shown. Fold down in half. Bring the three flaps on each side together while folding the section under each flap inward.

❻ Fold diagonally twice. Fold over and repeat on 5 remaining faces.

❼ Fold over the front and back flaps.

❾ Pull the center toward you.

❽ Repeat Step 6 on 5 remaining faces.

❿ Pulling it with one of your hands, fold over with the other hand.

⓫ Repeat Steps 8-9 on 5 remaining faces.

⓬ Separate the flaps evenly, and press the center down to spread out the petals. Make slits and form fine stamens.

Cut.

⓭ Finished stamens.

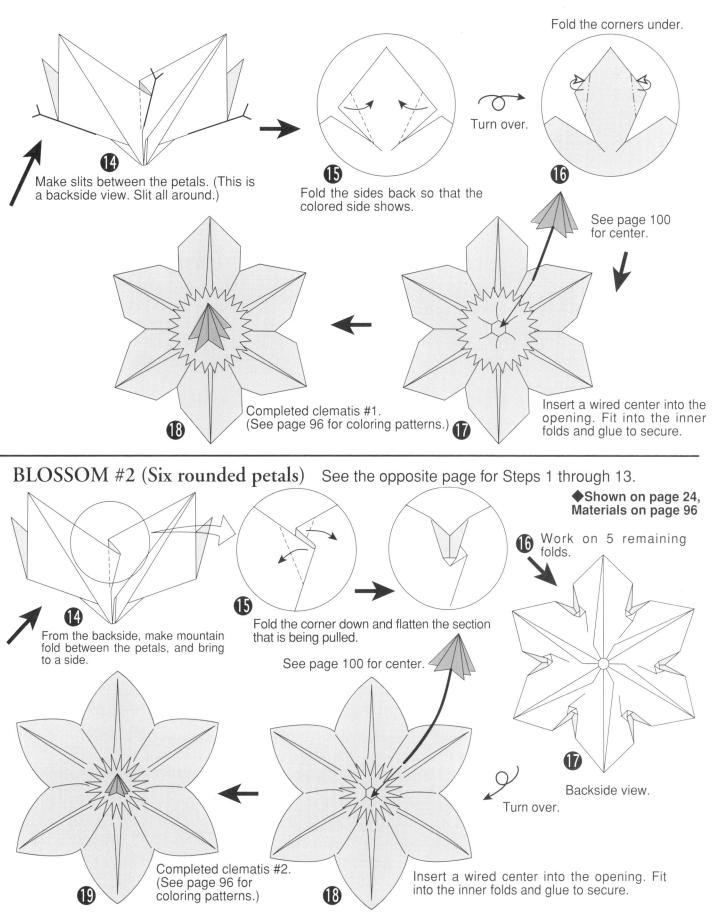

⑭ Make slits between the petals. (This is a backside view. Slit all around.)

⑮ Fold the sides back so that the colored side shows.

Turn over.

Fold the corners under.

⑯ See page 100 for center.

⑰ Insert a wired center into the opening. Fit into the inner folds and glue to secure.

⑱ Completed clematis #1. (See page 96 for coloring patterns.)

BLOSSOM #2 (Six rounded petals)   See the opposite page for Steps 1 through 13.

◆Shown on page 24, Materials on page 96

⑭ From the backside, make mountain fold between the petals, and bring to a side.

⑮ Fold the corner down and flatten the section that is being pulled.

See page 100 for center.

⑯ Work on 5 remaining folds.

⑰ Backside view. Turn over.

⑱ Insert a wired center into the opening. Fit into the inner folds and glue to secure.

⑲ Completed clematis #2. (See page 96 for coloring patterns.)

CENTER OF CLEMATIS #1/#2
(Work as for Steps 1 through 5 of BLOSSOM #1 on page 98, starting with plain side.)

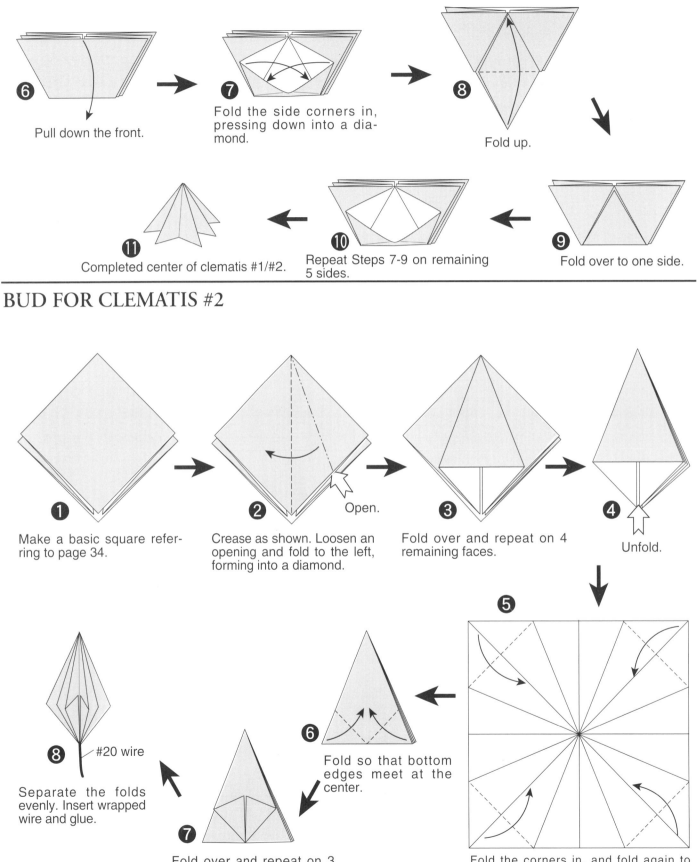

6 Pull down the front.

7 Fold the side corners in, pressing down into a diamond.

8 Fold up.

9 Fold over to one side.

10 Repeat Steps 7-9 on remaining 5 sides.

11 Completed center of clematis #1/#2.

BUD FOR CLEMATIS #2

1 Make a basic square referring to page 34.

2 Crease as shown. Loosen an opening and fold to the left, forming into a diamond. Open.

3 Fold over and repeat on 4 remaining faces.

4 Unfold.

5 Fold the corners in, and fold again to return to the previous step.

6 Fold so that bottom edges meet at the center.

7 Fold over and repeat on 3 remaining faces.

8 #20 wire
Separate the folds evenly. Insert wrapped wire and glue.

OPENING BLOSSOM FOR CLEMATIS #2
(Work as for BLOSSOM #2, Steps 1 through 10.)

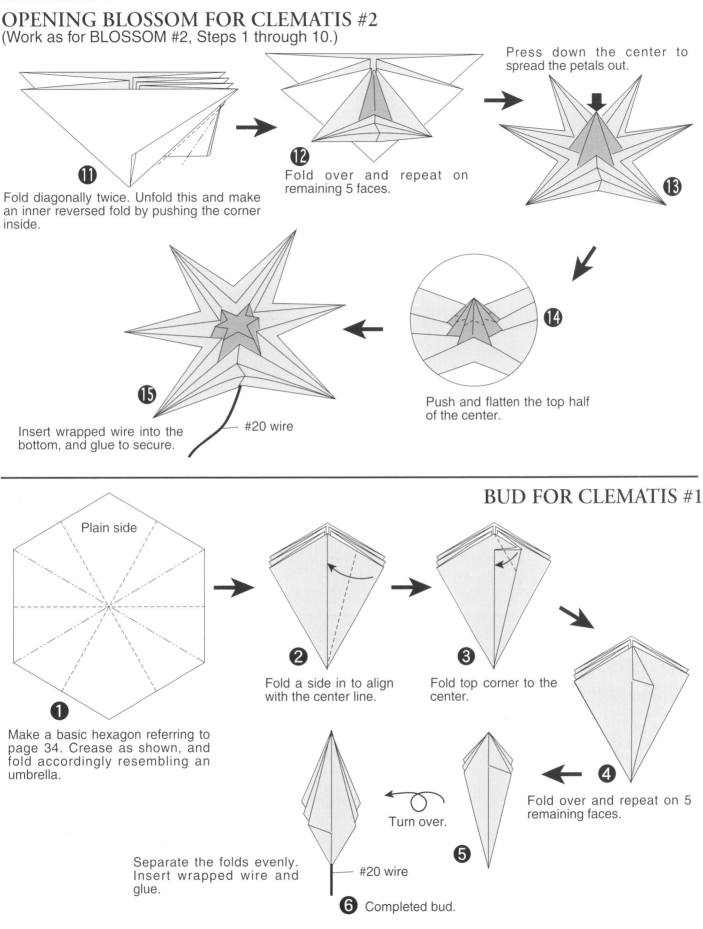

⑪ Fold diagonally twice. Unfold this and make an inner reversed fold by pushing the corner inside.

⑫ Fold over and repeat on remaining 5 faces.

Press down the center to spread the petals out.

⑬

⑭ Push and flatten the top half of the center.

⑮ Insert wrapped wire into the bottom, and glue to secure.

— #20 wire

BUD FOR CLEMATIS #1

Plain side

❶ Make a basic hexagon referring to page 34. Crease as shown, and fold accordingly resembling an umbrella.

❷ Fold a side in to align with the center line.

❸ Fold top corner to the center.

❹ Fold over and repeat on 5 remaining faces.

❺

Turn over.

Separate the folds evenly. Insert wrapped wire and glue.

— #20 wire

❻ Completed bud.

$\mathcal{LILY}$ (Shown on page 26)

Sheets of paper needed for each blossom, bud and calyx
Small blossom : 1 sheet (6", solid color)
Large blossom: *Washi* paper (10", white)
Bud   : 1 sheet (6", yellow-green)
Leaves   : *Washi* paper (green)
"Sheet" means a square sheet of origami or similar paper.

Other materials
Wrapped floral wire: #18 for stamens, #24 for leaves
1/8" thick wrapped floral wire (green)
Floral tape (beige, pale green, red, dark brown, white)
Alcohol-based marker

See page 112 for LEAF PATTERNS.

BLOSSOM

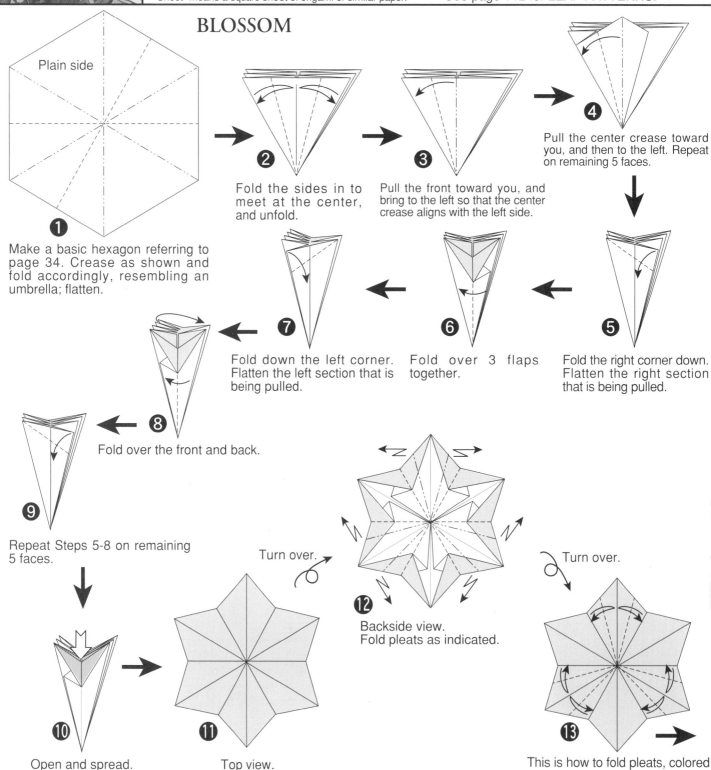

1 Make a basic hexagon referring to page 34. Crease as shown and fold accordingly, resembling an umbrella; flatten.

Plain side

2 Fold the sides in to meet at the center, and unfold.

3 Pull the front toward you, and bring to the left so that the center crease aligns with the left side.

4 Pull the center crease toward you, and then to the left. Repeat on remaining 5 faces.

5 Fold the right corner down. Flatten the right section that is being pulled.

6 Fold over 3 flaps together.

7 Fold down the left corner. Flatten the left section that is being pulled.

8 Fold over the front and back.

9 Repeat Steps 5-8 on remaining 5 faces.

10 Open and spread.

11 Top view.

Turn over.

12 Backside view. Fold pleats as indicated.

Turn over.

13 This is how to fold pleats, colored side up.

BUD

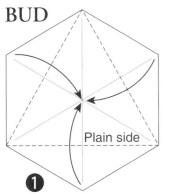

① Make a basic hexagon referring to page 34. Fold the corners to the center.

Plain side

② Make creases and fold into a diamond.

③ Crease by folding corners in so that bottom sides meet at the center and unfolding.

④ Push the corners in to make inner reversed folds.

⑤ Fold over one flap.

⑥ Fold sides to the center.

⑦ Fold over 2 flaps and repeat Step 6 on remaining 3 faces.

Rotate.

⑧ Fold over.

⑨ Arrange the shape for completed bud.

ASSEMBLY

Insert wire and glue. Tape down.

1/8" thick wrapped wire

Petals with more details (optional)

Pleat as for Step 13.

Make inner reversed folds all around.

⑭ This is how to fold pleats with colored side up.

Make a pistil and 6 stamens by wrapping each end of wire with floral tape.

3/8"

2½"

Stamens #18 wire

⑮

Pistil

3/8" floral tape

1/8" wire for stem

ASSEMBLY

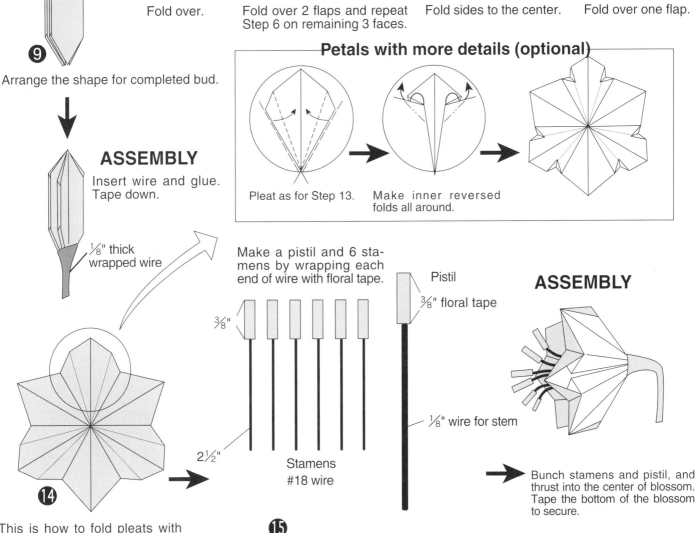

Bunch stamens and pistil, and thrust into the center of blossom. Tape the bottom of the blossom to secure.

CORNFLOWER (Shown on page 29)

Sheets of paper needed for each blossom
3 sheets of paper (6", shaded or solid color)
◆Pick combinations of matching colors such as purple/navy, white/lavender, and deep and light purple.

Other materials
#24 wrapped floral wire for stems

"Sheet" means a square sheet of origami or similar paper.

Work Steps 1 through 4 of basic octagon on page 35.

❶ Fold down.

❷ Unfold. Cut.
Cut along the folded flap to make a diamond.

❸ Turn upside down.

❹ Rotate.
Fold down the front flap.

❺ Crease as shown. Pulling the flap up, fold over to one side.

❻ Fold the back flap over. Repeat Steps 4-6 on 7 remaining faces.

❼ Insert your finger into the opening, and pull it toward you.

❽ Four right-hand flaps have been pulled out. Work on the left-hand flaps.

❾ Fold over the right half as shown,

❿ Glue.
Make 3 in the same manner, and glue them together.

⓫ Separate the petals evenly for completed blossom. Curl an end of wire, and pierce the center.

Changing the color of center

Glue.

Colored side

Work with another 6" sheet until Step 5. Fold up the lower half. Cut off the top. Unfold and glue to the center of blossom. Go back to the Step 6.

CHRYSANTHEMUM (Shown on page 29)

Sheets of paper needed for each flower
Blossom : 4 sheets (6", solid color)
Center   : 1 sheet (2", yellow)
Leaves   : *Washi* paper (green)

Other materials
Wrapped floral wire: #20 for stem, #24 for leaves
Floral tape (deep green)

"Sheet" means a square sheet of origami or similar paper.

See the opposite page for Steps 1 through 8 of CORNFLOWER.

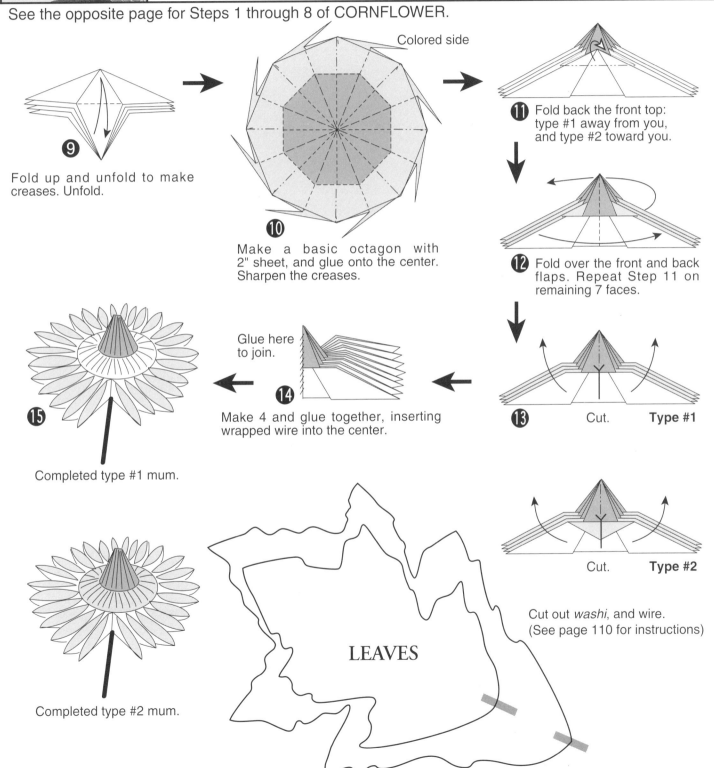

⑨ Fold up and unfold to make creases. Unfold.

Colored side

⑩ Make a basic octagon with 2" sheet, and glue onto the center. Sharpen the creases.

⑪ Fold back the front top: type #1 away from you, and type #2 toward you.

⑫ Fold over the front and back flaps. Repeat Step 11 on remaining 7 faces.

⑬ Cut. **Type #1**

Glue here to join.

⑭ Make 4 and glue together, inserting wrapped wire into the center.

⑮ Completed type #1 mum.

Completed type #2 mum.

Cut. **Type #2**

LEAVES

Cut out *washi*, and wire. (See page 110 for instructions)

105

BALLOON FLOWER (Shown on page 31)

Sheets of paper needed for each flower and bud
Blossom : 2 sheets (6", both shaded and solid color)
Bud   : 1 sheet (6", shaded color)
Leaves : *Washi* paper (green)

Other materials
Wrapped floral wire: #20 for stem, #24 for leaf
Floral tape (both green and deep green)

"Sheet" means a square sheet of origami or similar paper.

BLOSSOM #1 (Paste two sheets, plain sides in.)

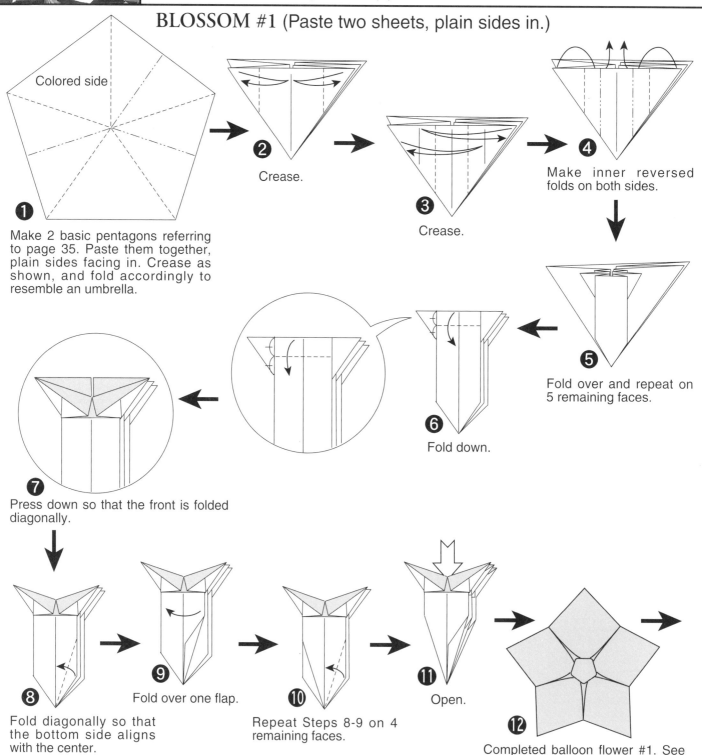

1 Make 2 basic pentagons referring to page 35. Paste them together, plain sides facing in. Crease as shown, and fold accordingly to resemble an umbrella.

Colored side

2 Crease.

3 Crease.

4 Make inner reversed folds on both sides.

5 Fold over and repeat on 5 remaining faces.

6 Fold down.

7 Press down so that the front is folded diagonally.

8 Fold diagonally so that the bottom side aligns with the center.

9 Fold over one flap.

10 Repeat Steps 8-9 on 4 remaining faces.

11 Open.

12 Completed balloon flower #1. See the opposite page for assembly.

106

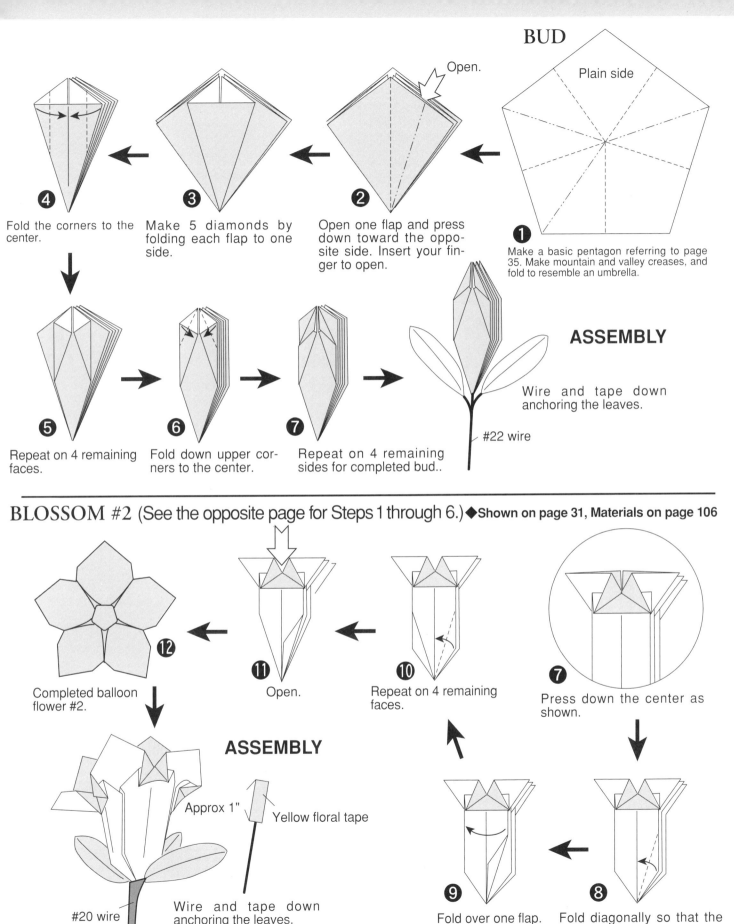

BUD

Plain side

① Make a basic pentagon referring to page 35. Make mountain and valley creases, and fold to resemble an umbrella.

Open.

② Open one flap and press down toward the opposite side. Insert your finger to open.

③ Make 5 diamonds by folding each flap to one side.

④ Fold the corners to the center.

⑤ Repeat on 4 remaining faces.

⑥ Fold down upper corners to the center.

⑦ Repeat on 4 remaining sides for completed bud..

ASSEMBLY

Wire and tape down anchoring the leaves.

#22 wire

BLOSSOM #2 (See the opposite page for Steps 1 through 6.) ◆Shown on page 31, Materials on page 106

⑫ Completed balloon flower #2.

⑪ Open.

⑩ Repeat on 4 remaining faces.

⑦ Press down the center as shown.

⑨ Fold over one flap.

⑧ Fold diagonally so that the bottom sides align with the center.

ASSEMBLY

Approx 1"   Yellow floral tape

Wire and tape down anchoring the leaves.

#20 wire

CYCLAMEN (Shown on page 32)

Sheets of paper needed for each flower and bud
Blossom : 1 sheet (6", white paper or pink *washi*)
Bud : 1 sheet (3", white paper or pink *washi*)
Calyx(cup) : 1 sheet (2", deep green)
Leaves : *Washi* paper (green)

Other materials
Wrapped floral wire: #20 for stem, #24 for leaf
Floral tape (yellow, red or beige)
Alcohol-based markers

"Sheet" means a square sheet of origami or similar paper.

BLOSSOM

1 Plain side

Make a basic pentagon referring to page 35. Make mountain and valley creases as shown, and fold to resemble an umbrella.

2 Open.

Open one flap and press down toward the opposite side. Insert your finger to open.

3

Make 5 diamonds by folding each flap to one side.

4 Crease at a quarter length from the bottom. Unfold.

5 Valley fold · Plain side

Crease again as shown. Pushing the center inward, fold to resemble an umbrella.

6

Fold the side corners in.

7

Fold bottom corners in.

8

Fold over and repeat Steps 6-7 on 4 remaining faces.

9

Open the petals, flattening the smooth faces.

10

Completed blossom #1.

In Step 6, push the corners inside (inner reversed folds).

Completed blossom #2.

In Step 5, color the center polygon.
In Step 6, make inner reversed folds.

Completed blossom #3.

BUD

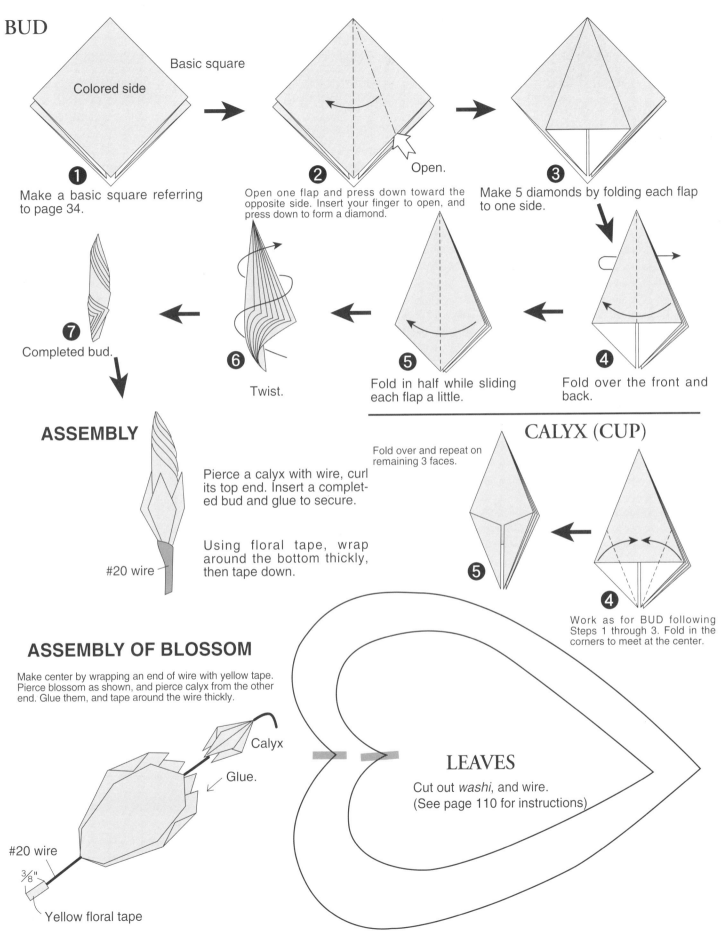

1 Make a basic square referring to page 34.

Colored side

Basic square

2 Open one flap and press down toward the opposite side. Insert your finger to open, and press down to form a diamond.

Open.

3 Make 5 diamonds by folding each flap to one side.

4 Fold over the front and back.

5 Fold in half while sliding each flap a little.

6 Twist.

7 Completed bud.

ASSEMBLY

Pierce a calyx with wire, curl its top end. Insert a completed bud and glue to secure.

Using floral tape, wrap around the bottom thickly, then tape down.

#20 wire

CALYX (CUP)

Fold over and repeat on remaining 3 faces.

5

4 Work as for BUD following Steps 1 through 3. Fold in the corners to meet at the center.

ASSEMBLY OF BLOSSOM

Make center by wrapping an end of wire with yellow tape. Pierce blossom as shown, and pierce calyx from the other end. Glue them, and tape around the wire thickly.

Calyx

Glue.

#20 wire

3/8"

Yellow floral tape

LEAVES

Cut out *washi*, and wire.
(See page 110 for instructions)

ACTUAL SIZE LEAF PATTERNS

Make a template by either photocopying or tracing each pattern. Place it on the layered *washi* paper, and cut out the shape. Glue a piece of wrapped floral wire onto the center of each leaf, and adjust the length of wire, so that it extends about 3" from the bottom of the leaf. Make an appropriate number of leaves and join each to the stem of flower using floral tape.

★**Helpful Hint:** Since there are several "typical" leafing patterns, it is important to observe actual flowers, and learn how to attach the leaves to resemble the flower's natural leafing and branching tendencies.

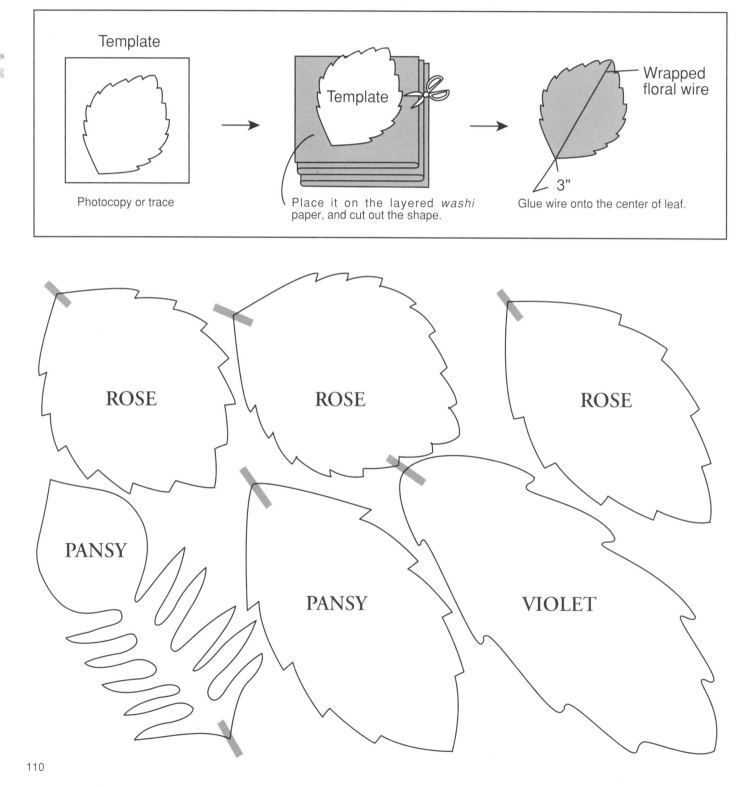

ROSE

ROSE

ROSE

PANSY

PANSY

VIOLET

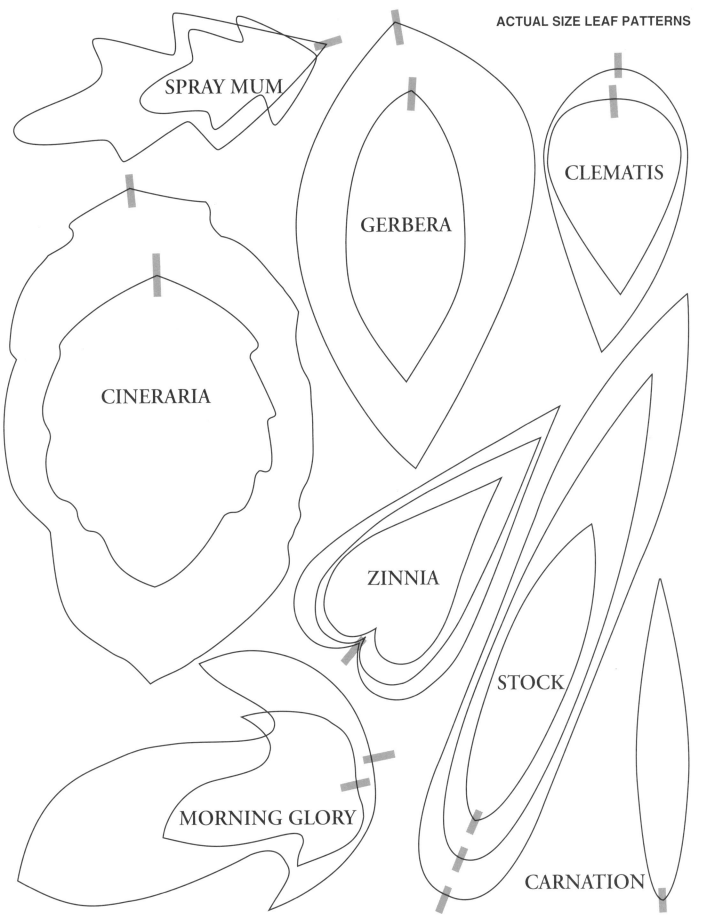

SPRAY MUM

GERBERA

CLEMATIS

CINERARIA

ZINNIA

STOCK

MORNING GLORY

CARNATION

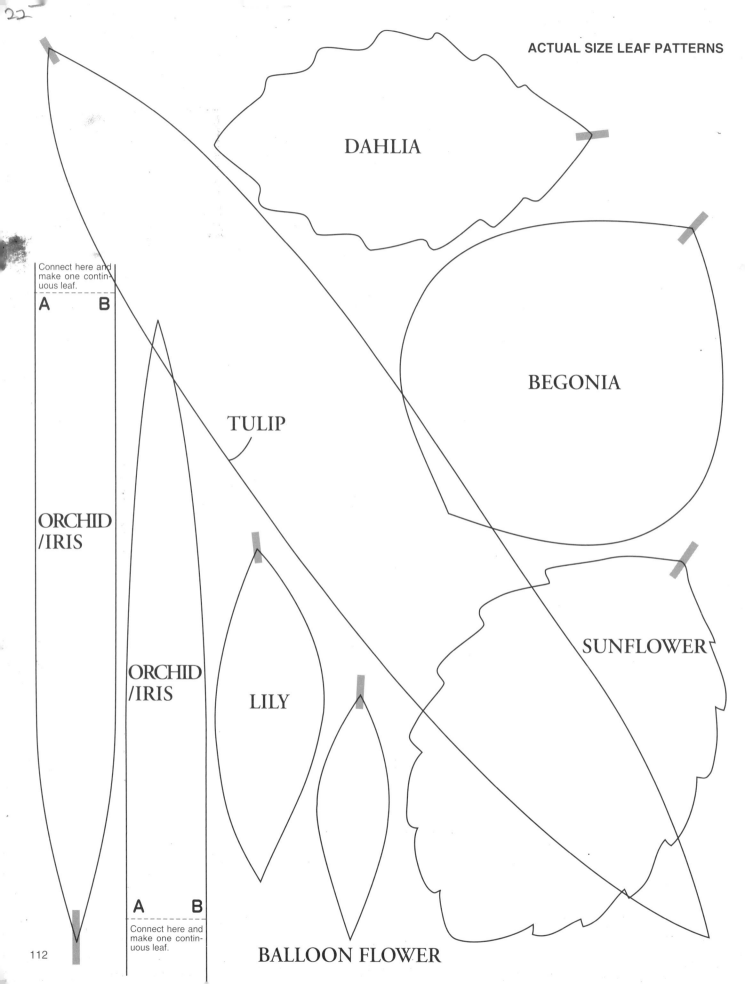

DAHLIA

BEGONIA

Connect here and make one continuous leaf.

A   B

TULIP

ORCHID/IRIS

ORCHID/IRIS

SUNFLOWER

LILY

A   B

Connect here and make one continuous leaf.

BALLOON FLOWER